FOREWORD

The collection of "Everything Will Be Okay" travel phrasebooks published by T&P Books is designed for people traveling abroad for tourism and business. The phrasebooks contain what matters most - the essentials for basic communication. This is an indispensable set of phrases to "survive" while abroad.

This phrasebook will help you in most cases where you need to ask something, get directions, find out how much something costs, etc. It can also resolve difficult communication situations where gestures just won't help.

This book contains a lot of phrases that have been grouped according to the most relevant topics. A separate section of the book also provides a small dictionary with more than 1,500 important and useful words.

Take "Everything Will Be Okay" phrasebook with you on the road and you'll have an irreplaceable traveling companion who will help you find your way out of any situation and teach you to not fear speaking with foreigners.

TABLE OF CONTENTS

T&P Books Publishing

T&P Books Publishing

PHRASEBOOK

— GERMAN —

THE MOST IMPORTANT PHRASES

This phrasebook contains
the most important
phrases and questions
for basic communication
Everything you need
to survive overseas

By Andrey Taranov

T&P BOOKS

Phrasebook + 1500-word dictionary

English-German phrasebook & concise dictionary

By Andrey Taranov

The collection of "Everything Will Be Okay" travel phrasebooks published by T&P Books is designed for people traveling abroad for tourism and business. The phrasebooks contain what matters most - the essentials for basic communication. This is an indispensable set of phrases to "survive" while abroad.

Another section of the book also provides a small dictionary with more than 1,500 useful words arranged alphabetically. The dictionary includes a lot of gastronomic terms and will be helpful when ordering food at a restaurant or buying groceries at the store.

T&P Books Publishing
www.tpbooks.com

ISBN: 978-1-78767-226-0

This book is also available in E-book formats.
Please visit www.tpbooks.com or the major online bookstores.

PRONUNCIATION

T&P phonetic alphabet	German example	English example

Vowels

[a]	Blatt	shorter than in ask
[ɐ]	Meister	nut
[e]	Melodie	elm, medal
[ɛ]	Herbst	man, bad
[ə]	Leuchte	driver, teacher
[ɔ]	Knopf	bottle, doctor
[o]	Operette	pod, John
[œ]	Förster	German Hölle
[ø]	nötig	eternal, church
[æ]	Los Angeles	candle, lamp
[i]	Spiel	shorter than in feet
[ɪ]	Absicht	big, America
[ʊ]	Skulptur	good, booklet
[u]	Student	book
[y]	Pyramide	fuel, tuna
[ʏ]	Eukalyptus	fuel, tuna

Consonants

[b]	Bibel	baby, book
[d]	Dorf	day, doctor
[f]	Elefant	face, food
[ʒ]	Ingenieur	forge, pleasure
[dʒ]	Jeans	joke, general
[j]	Interview	yes, New York
[g]	August	game, gold
[h]	Haare	home, have
[ç]	glücklich	humor
[x]	Kochtopf	as in Scots 'loch'
[k]	Kaiser	clock, kiss
[l]	Verlag	lace, people

T&P phonetic alphabet	German example	English example
[m]	**Messer**	magic, milk
[n]	**Norden**	name, normal
[ŋ]	**Onkel**	English, ring
[p]	**Gespräch**	pencil, private
[r]	**Force majeure**	rice, radio
[ʁ]	**Kirche**	French (guttural) R
[ʀ]	**fragen**	uvular vibrant [r]
[s]	**Fenster**	city, boss
[t]	**Foto**	tourist, trip
[ts]	**Gesetz**	cats, tsetse fly
[ʃ]	**Anschlag**	machine, shark
[tʃ]	**Deutsche**	church, French
[w]	**Sweater**	vase, winter
[v]	**Antwort**	very, river
[z]	**langsam**	zebra, please

Diphthongs

[aɪ]	**Speicher**	tie, driver
[ɪa]	**Miniatur**	Kenya, piano
[ɪo]	**Radio**	New York
[jo]	**Illustration**	New York
[ɔɪ]	**feucht**	oil, boy, point
[ɪe]	**Karriere**	yesterday, yen

Other symbols used in transcription

[']	['aːbə]	primary stress
[ˌ]	['dɛŋkˌmaːl]	secondary stress
[ʔ]	[oˈliːvənˌʔøːl]	glottal stop
[ː]	['myːlə]	long-vowel mark
[·]	['ʀaɪzə·byˌʀoː]	interpunct

LIST OF ABBREVIATIONS

English abbreviations

ab.	-	about
adj	-	adjective
adv	-	adverb
anim.	-	animate
as adj	-	attributive noun used as adjective
e.g.	-	for example
etc.	-	et cetera
fam.	-	familiar
fem.	-	feminine
form.	-	formal
inanim.	-	inanimate
masc.	-	masculine
math	-	mathematics
mil.	-	military
n	-	noun
pl	-	plural
pron.	-	pronoun
sb	-	somebody
sing.	-	singular
sth	-	something
v aux	-	auxiliary verb
vi	-	intransitive verb
vi, vt	-	intransitive, transitive verb
vt	-	transitive verb

German abbreviations

f	-	feminine noun
f pl	-	feminine plural
f, n	-	feminine, neuter
m	-	masculine noun
m pl	-	masculine plural
m, f	-	masculine, feminine
m, n	-	masculine, neuter
n	-	neuter
n pl	-	neuter plural

pl	-	plural
v mod	-	modal verb
vi	-	intransitive verb
vi, vt	-	intransitive, transitive verb
vt	-	transitive verb

T&P BOOKS

GERMAN
PHRASEBOOK

This section contains
important phrases that may
come in handy in various
real-life situations.
The phrasebook will help
you ask for directions, clarify
a price, buy tickets, and
order food at a restaurant

T&P Books Publishing

PHRASEBOOK
CONTENTS

T&P Books Publishing

The bare minimum

Excuse me, ...

Entschuldigen Sie bitte, ...
[ɛnt'ʃʊldɪgən zi: 'bɪtə, ...]

Hello.

Hallo.
[ha'lo:]

Thank you.

Danke.
[daŋkə]

Good bye.

Auf Wiedersehen.
[aʊf 'vi:dɐˌze:ən]

Yes.

Ja.
[ja:]

No.

Nein.
[naɪn]

I don't know.

Ich weiß nicht.
[ɪç vaɪs nɪçt]

Where? | Where to? | When?

Wo? | Wohin? | Wann?
[vo:? | vo'hɪn? | van?]

I need ...

Ich brauche ...
[ɪç 'bʀaʊxə ...]

I want ...

Ich möchte ...
[ɪç 'mœçtə ...]

Do you have ...?

Haben Sie ...?
[ha:bən zi: ...?]

Is there a ... here?

Gibt es hier ...?
[gi:pt ɛs hi:ɐ ...?]

May I ...?

Kann ich ...?
[kan ɪç ...?]

..., please (polite request)

Bitte
[bɪtə]

I'm looking for ...

Ich suche ...
[ɪç 'zu:xə ...]

the restroom

Toilette
[toa'lɛtə]

an ATM

Geldautomat
[gɛlt?aʊtoˌma:t]

a pharmacy (drugstore)

Apotheke
[apo'te:kə]

a hospital

Krankenhaus
[kʀaŋkənˌhaʊs]

the police station

Polizeistation
[poli'tsaɪ·ʃtaˌtsjo:n]

the subway

U-Bahn
[u:ba:n]

a taxi	**Taxi** [taksi]
the train station	**Bahnhof** [baːnˌhoːf]

My name is ...	**Ich heiße ...** [ɪç ˈhaɪsə ...]
What's your name?	**Wie heißen Sie?** [viː ˈhaɪsən ziː?]
Could you please help me?	**Helfen Sie mir bitte.** [hɛlfən ziː miːɐ ˈbɪtə]
I've got a problem.	**Ich habe ein Problem.** [ɪç ˈhaːbə aɪn pʀoˈbleːm]
I don't feel well.	**Mir ist schlecht.** [miːɐ ɪs ʃlɛçt]
Call an ambulance!	**Rufen Sie einen Krankenwagen!** [ʀuːfən ziː ˈaɪnən ˈkʀaŋkənˌvaːgən!]
May I make a call?	**Darf ich telefonieren?** [daʁf ɪç telefoˈniːʀən?]

I'm sorry.	**Entschuldigung.** [ɛntˈʃʊldɪgʊŋ]
You're welcome.	**Keine Ursache.** [kaɪnə ˈuːɐˌzaχə]

I, me	**ich** [ɪç]
you (inform.)	**du** [duː]
he	**er** [eːɐ]
she	**sie** [ziː]
they (masc.)	**sie** [ziː]
they (fem.)	**sie** [ziː]
we	**wir** [viːɐ]
you (pl)	**ihr** [iːɐ]
you (sg, form.)	**Sie** [ziː]

ENTRANCE	**EINGANG** [aɪnˌgaŋ]
EXIT	**AUSGANG** [aʊsˌgaŋ]
OUT OF ORDER	**AUßER BETRIEB** [ˌaʊsə bəˈtʀiːp]
CLOSED	**GESCHLOSSEN** [gəˈʃlɔsən]

OPEN

OFFEN
[ɔfən]

FOR WOMEN

FÜR DAMEN
[fyːɐ 'damən]

FOR MEN

FÜR HERREN
[fyːɐ 'hɛʀən]

Questions

Where?	**Wo?** [vo:?]
Where to?	**Wohin?** [vo'hɪn?]
Where from?	**Woher?** [vo'heːɐ?]
Why?	**Warum?** [va'ʀʊm?]
For what reason?	**Wozu?** [vo'tsuː?]
When?	**Wann?** [van?]

How long?	**Wie lange?** [viː 'laŋə?]
At what time?	**Um wie viel Uhr?** [ʊm viː fiːl uːɐ?]
How much?	**Wie viel?** [viː fiːl?]
Do you have ...?	**Haben Sie ...?** [haːbən ziː ...?]
Where is ...?	**Wo befindet sich ...?** [vo: bə'fɪndət zɪç ...?]

What time is it?	**Wie spät ist es?** [viː ʃpɛːt ist ɛs?]
May I make a call?	**Darf ich telefonieren?** [daʀf ɪç telefo'niːʀən?]
Who's there?	**Wer ist da?** [veːɐ ist daː?]
Can I smoke here?	**Darf ich hier rauchen?** [daʀf ɪç hiːɐ 'ʀaʊxən?]
May I ...?	**Darf ich ...?** [daʀf ɪç ...?]

Needs

I'd like ...	**Ich hätte gerne ...** [ɪç 'hɛtə 'gɛʀnə ...]
I don't want ...	**Ich will nicht ...** [ɪç vɪl nɪçt ...]
I'm thirsty.	**Ich habe Durst.** [ɪç 'haːbə dʊʀst]
I want to sleep.	**Ich möchte schlafen.** [ɪç 'mœçtə 'ʃlaːfən]
I want ...	**Ich möchte ...** [ɪç 'mœçtə ...]
to wash up	**abwaschen** [ap'vaʃən]
to brush my teeth	**meine Zähne putzen** [maɪnə 'tsɛːnə 'pʊtsən]
to rest a while	**eine Weile ausruhen** [aɪnə 'vaɪlə 'aʊsˌʀuːən]
to change my clothes	**meine Kleidung wechseln** [maɪnə 'klaɪdʊŋ 'vɛksəln]
to go back to the hotel	**zurück ins Hotel gehen** [tsu'ʀʏk ɪns ho'tɛl 'geːən]
to buy ...	**... kaufen** [... 'kaʊfən]
to go to ...	**... gehen** [... 'geːən]
to visit ...	**... besuchen** [... bə'zuχən]
to meet with ...	**... treffen** [... 'tʀɛfən]
to make a call	**einen Anruf tätigen** [aɪnən 'anˌʀuːf 'tɛːtɪgən]
I'm tired.	**Ich bin müde.** [ɪç bɪn 'myːdə]
We are tired.	**Wir sind müde.** [viːɐ zɪnt 'myːdə]
I'm cold.	**Mir ist kalt.** [miːɐ ɪs kalt]
I'm hot.	**Mir ist heiß.** [miːɐ ɪs haɪs]
I'm OK.	**Mir passt es.** [miːɐ past ɛs]

I need to make a call.

Ich muss telefonieren.
[ɪç mʊs telefo'niːʀən]

I need to go to the restroom.

Ich muss auf die Toilette.
[ɪç mʊs 'aʊf di toa'lɛtə]

I have to go.

Ich muss gehen.
[ɪç mʊs 'geːən]

I have to go now.

Ich muss jetzt gehen.
[ɪç mʊs jɛtst 'geːən]

Asking for directions

Excuse me, ...	**Entschuldigen Sie bitte, ...** [ɛntˈʃuldɪgən ziː ˈbɪtə, ...]
Where is ...?	**Wo befindet sich ...?** [voː bəˈfɪndət zɪç ...?]
Which way is ...?	**Welcher Weg ist ...?** [vɛlçə veːk ist ...?]
Could you help me, please?	**Könnten Sie mir bitte helfen?** [kœntən ziː miːɐ ˈbɪtə ˈhɛlfən?]

I'm looking for ...	**Ich suche ...** [ɪç ˈzuːχə ...]
I'm looking for the exit.	**Ich suche den Ausgang.** [ɪç ˈzuːχə den ˈaʊsˌgaŋ]
I'm going to ...	**Ich fahre nach ...** [ɪç ˈfaːʀə naːχ ...]
Am I going the right way to ...?	**Gehe ich richtig nach ...?** [geːə ɪç ˈʀɪçtɪç naːχ ...?]

Is it far?	**Ist es weit?** [ist ɛs vaɪt?]
Can I get there on foot?	**Kann ich dort zu Fuß hingehen?** [kan ɪç dɔʀt tsu fuːs ˈhɪnˌgeːən?]
Can you show me on the map?	**Können Sie es mir auf der Karte zeigen?** [kœnən ziː ɛs miːɐ aʊf deːɐ ˈkaʀtə ˈtsaɪgən?]
Show me where we are right now.	**Zeigen Sie mir wo wir gerade sind.** [tsaɪgən ziː miːɐ voː viːɐ gəˈʀaːdə zɪnt]

Here	**Hier** [hiːɐ]
There	**Dort** [dɔʀt]
This way	**Hierher** [hiːɐˈheːɐ]

Turn right.	**Biegen Sie rechts ab.** [biːgən ziː ʀɛçts ap]
Turn left.	**Biegen Sie links ab.** [biːgən ziː lɪŋks ap]
first (second, third) turn	**erste (zweite, dritte) Abzweigung** [ɛʀstə (ˈtsvaɪtə, ˈdʀɪtə) ˈapˌtsvaɪguŋ]
to the right	**nach rechts** [naːχ ʀɛçts]

to the left

nach links
[na:χ lɪŋks]

Go straight ahead.

Laufen Sie geradeaus.
[laʊfən zi: gəʀa:də'ʔaʊs]

Signs

WELCOME!	**HERZLICH WILLKOMMEN!** [hɛʁtslɪç vɪlˈkɔmən!]
ENTRANCE	**EINGANG** [aɪnˌgaŋ]
EXIT	**AUSGANG** [aʊsˌgaŋ]
PUSH	**DRÜCKEN** [dʀʏkən]
PULL	**ZIEHEN** [tsiːən]
OPEN	**OFFEN** [ɔfən]
CLOSED	**GESCHLOSSEN** [gəˈʃlɔsən]
FOR WOMEN	**FÜR DAMEN** [fyːɐ ˈdamən]
FOR MEN	**FÜR HERREN** [fyːɐ ˈhɛʀən]
GENTLEMEN, GENTS	**HERREN-WC** [hɛʀən-veˈtseː]
WOMEN	**DAMEN-WC** [daːmən-veˈtseː]
DISCOUNTS	**RABATT	REDUZIERT** [ʀaˈbat	ʀeduˈtsiːɐt]
SALE	**AUSVERKAUF** [aʊsfɛɐˌkaʊf]
FREE	**GRATIS** [gʀaːtɪs]
NEW!	**NEU!** [nɔɪ!]
ATTENTION!	**ACHTUNG!** [aχtʊŋ!]
NO VACANCIES	**KEINE ZIMMER FREI** [kaɪnə ˈtsɪmɐ fʀaɪ]
RESERVED	**RESERVIERT** [ʀezɛʀˈviːɐt]
ADMINISTRATION	**VERWALTUNG** [fɛɐˈvaltʊŋ]
STAFF ONLY	**NUR FÜR PERSONAL** [nuːɐ fyːɐ pɛʀzoˈnaːl]

BEWARE OF THE DOG!	**BISSIGER HUND** [bɪsɪge hʊnt]
NO SMOKING!	**RAUCHEN VERBOTEN** [ʀaʊχən fɛɐ'boːtən]
DO NOT TOUCH!	**NICHT ANFASSEN!** [nɪçt 'anfasən!]
DANGEROUS	**GEFÄHRLICH** [gə'fɛːɐlɪç]
DANGER	**GEFAHR** [gə'faːɐ]
HIGH VOLTAGE	**HOCHSPANNUNG** [hoːχˌʃpanʊŋ]
NO SWIMMING!	**BADEN VERBOTEN** [baːdən fɛɐ'boːtən]

OUT OF ORDER	**AUßER BETRIEB** [ˌaʊsɐ bə'tʀiːp]
FLAMMABLE	**LEICHTENTZÜNDLICH** [laɪçt?ɛn'tsʏntlɪç]
FORBIDDEN	**VERBOTEN** [fɛɐ'boːtən]
NO TRESPASSING!	**DURCHGANG VERBOTEN** [dʊʀçˌgaŋ fɛɐ'boːtən]
WET PAINT	**FRISCH GESTRICHEN** [fʀɪʃ gə'ʃtʀɪçən]

CLOSED FOR RENOVATIONS	**WEGEN RENOVIERUNG GESCHLOSSEN** [veːgən ʀeno'viːʀʊŋ gə'ʃlɔsən]
WORKS AHEAD	**ACHTUNG BAUARBEITEN** [aχtʊŋ 'baʊ?aʀˌbaɪtən]
DETOUR	**UMLEITUNG** [ʊmˌlaɪtʊŋ]

Transportation. General phrases

plane	**Flugzeug**
	[flu:k‚tsɔɪk]
train	**Zug**
	[tsu:k]
bus	**Bus**
	[bʊs]
ferry	**Fähre**
	[fɛ:ʀə]
taxi	**Taxi**
	[taksi]
car	**Auto**
	[aʊto]

schedule	**Zeitplan**
	[tsaɪt‚pla:n]
Where can I see the schedule?	**Wo kann ich den Zeitplan sehen?**
	[vo: kan ɪç den 'tsaɪt‚pla:n 'ze:ən?]
workdays (weekdays)	**Arbeitstage**
	[aʀbaɪts‚ta:gə]
weekends	**Wochenenden**
	[vɔχən‚ʔɛndən]
holidays	**Ferien**
	[fe:ʀɪən]

DEPARTURE	**ABFLUG**
	[apflu:k]
ARRIVAL	**ANKUNFT**
	[ankʊnft]
DELAYED	**VERSPÄTET**
	[fɛɐ'ʃpɛ:tət]
CANCELLED	**GESTRICHEN**
	[gə'ʃtʀɪçən]

next (train, etc.)	**nächster**
	[nɛ:çstə]
first	**erster**
	[e:ɐstə]
last	**letzter**
	[lɛtstə]

When is the next ...?	**Wann kommt der nächste ...?**
	[van kɔmt de:ɐ 'nɛ:çstə ...?]
When is the first ...?	**Wann kommt der erste ...?**
	[van kɔmt de:ɐ 'ɛʀstə ...?]

When is the last ...?

Wann kommt der letzte ...?
[van kɔmt deːɐ 'lɛtstə ...?]

transfer (change of trains, etc.)

Transfer
[tʀans'feːɐ]

to make a transfer

einen Transfer machen
[aɪnən tʀans'feːɐ 'maxən]

Do I need to make a transfer?

Muss ich einen Transfer machen?
[mʊs ɪç 'aɪnən tʀans'feːɐ 'maxən?]

Buying tickets

Where can I buy tickets?	**Wo kann ich Fahrkarten kaufen?** [vo: kan ɪç 'fa:ɐ̯ˌkaʁtən 'kaʊfən?]
ticket	**Fahrkarte** [fa:ɐ̯ˌkaʁtə]
to buy a ticket	**Eine Fahrkarte kaufen** [aɪnə 'fa:ɐ̯ˌkaʁtə 'kaʊfən]
ticket price	**Fahrpreis** [fa:ɐ̯ˌpʀaɪs]
Where to?	**Wohin?** [vo'hɪn?]
To what station?	**Welche Station?** [vɛlçə ʃta'tsjo:n?]
I need ...	**Ich brauche ...** [ɪç 'bʀaʊχə ...]
one ticket	**eine Fahrkarte** [aɪnə 'fa:ɐ̯ˌkaʁtə]
two tickets	**zwei Fahrkarten** [tsvaɪ 'fa:ɐ̯ˌkaʁtən]
three tickets	**drei Fahrkarten** [dʀaɪ 'fa:ɐ̯ˌkaʁtən]
one-way	**in eine Richtung** [ɪn 'aɪnə 'ʀɪçtʊŋ]
round-trip	**hin und zurück** [hɪn ʊnt tsu'ʀʏk]
first class	**erste Klasse** [ɛʁstə 'klasə]
second class	**zweite Klasse** [tsvaɪtə 'klasə]
today	**heute** [hɔɪtə]
tomorrow	**morgen** [mɔʁgən]
the day after tomorrow	**übermorgen** [y:bɐˌmɔʁgən]
in the morning	**am Vormittag** [am 'fo:ɐmɪta:k]
in the afternoon	**am Nachmittag** [am 'na:χmɪˌta:k]
in the evening	**am Abend** [am 'a:bənt]

aisle seat

Gangplatz
[gaŋˌplats]

window seat

Fensterplatz
[fɛnstɐˌplats]

How much?

Wie viel?
[vi: fi:l?]

Can I pay by credit card?

Kann ich mit Karte zahlen?
[kan ɪç mɪt 'kaʁtə 'tsa:lən?]

Bus

bus	**Bus** [bʊs]
intercity bus	**Fernbus** [fɛʁnbʊs]
bus stop	**Bushaltestelle** [bʊshaltəˌʃtɛlə]
Where's the nearest bus stop?	**Wo ist die nächste Bushaltestelle?** [voː ist di ˈnɛːçstə ˈbʊshaltəˌʃtɛlə?]
number (bus ~, etc.)	**Nummer** [nʊmɐ]
Which bus do I take to get to …?	**Welchen Bus nehme ich um** **nach … zu kommen?** [vɛlçən bʊs ˈneːmə ɪç ʊm naːx … tsu ˈkɔmən?]
Does this bus go to …?	**Fährt dieser Bus nach …?** [fɛːɐt ˈdiːzɐ bʊs naːx …?]
How frequent are the buses?	**Wie oft fahren die Busse?** [viː ɔft ˈfaːʁən di ˈbʊsə?]
every 15 minutes	**alle fünfzehn Minuten** [alə ˈfʏnftseːn miˈnuːtən]
every half hour	**jede halbe Stunde** [jeːdə ˈhalbə ˈʃtʊndə]
every hour	**jede Stunde** [jeːdə ˈʃtʊndə]
several times a day	**mehrmals täglich** [meːɐmaːls ˈtɛːklɪç]
… times a day	**… Mal am Tag** [… mal am taːk]
schedule	**Zeitplan** [tsaɪtˌplaːn]
Where can I see the schedule?	**Wo kann ich den Zeitplan sehen?** [voː kan ɪç den ˈtsaɪtˌplaːn ˈzeːən?]
When is the next bus?	**Wann kommt der nächste Bus?** [van kɔmt deːɐ ˈnɛːçstə bʊs?]
When is the first bus?	**Wann kommt der erste Bus?** [van kɔmt deːɐ ˈɛʁstə bʊs?]
When is the last bus?	**Wann kommt der letzte Bus?** [van kɔmt deːɐ ˈlɛtstə bʊs?]

stop	**Halt** [halt]
next stop	**nächster Halt** [nɛ:çstɐ halt]
last stop (terminus)	**letzter Halt** [lɛtstɐ halt]
Stop here, please.	**Halten Sie hier bitte an.** [haltən zi: hi:ɐ 'bɪtə an]
Excuse me, this is my stop.	**Entschuldigen Sie mich, dies ist meine Haltestelle.** [ɛnt'ʃʊldɪgən zi: mɪç, di:s ist maɪnə 'haltəʃtɛlə]

Train

train	**Zug** [tsuːk]
suburban train	**S-Bahn** [ɛsˌbaːn]
long-distance train	**Fernzug** [fɛʁnˌtsuːk]
train station	**Bahnhof** [baːnˌhoːf]
Excuse me, where is the exit to the platform?	**Entschuldigen Sie bitte,** **wo ist der Ausgang zum Bahngleis?** [ɛntˈʃʊldɪgən ziː 'bɪtə, voː ist deːɐ 'aʊsgaŋ tsʊm 'baːnˌglaɪs?]

Does this train go to …?	**Fährt dieser Zug nach …?** [fɛːɐt 'diːzɐ tsuːk naːχ …?]
next train	**nächster Zug** [nɛːçstɐ tsuːk]
When is the next train?	**Wann kommt der nächste Zug?** [van kɔmt deːɐ 'nɛːçstə tsuːk?]
Where can I see the schedule?	**Wo kann ich den Zeitplan sehen?** [voː kan ɪç den 'tsaɪtˌplaːn 'zeːən?]
From which platform?	**Von welchem Bahngleis?** [fɔn 'vɛlχəm 'baːnˌglaɪs?]
When does the train arrive in …?	**Wann kommt der Zug in … an?** [van kɔmt deːɐ tsuːk ɪn … an?]

Please help me.	**Helfen Sie mir bitte.** [hɛlfən ziː miːɐ 'bɪtə]
I'm looking for my seat.	**Ich suche meinen Platz.** [ɪç 'zuːχə 'maɪnən plats]
We're looking for our seats.	**Wir suchen unsere Plätze.** [viːɐ 'zuːχən 'ʊnzərə 'plɛtsə]

My seat is taken.	**Unser Platz ist besetzt.** [ʊnzɐ plats ist bə'zɛtst]
Our seats are taken.	**Unsere Plätze sind besetzt.** [ʊnzərə 'plɛtsə zɪnt bə'zɛtst]
I'm sorry but this is my seat.	**Entschuldigen Sie,** **aber das ist mein Platz.** [ɛntˈʃʊldɪgən ziː, 'aːbɐ das ist maɪn plats]

Is this seat taken?

Ist der Platz frei?
[ist deːɐ plats fʁaɪ?]

May I sit here?

Darf ich mich hier setzen?
[daʁf ɪç mɪç hiːɐ 'zɛtsən?]

On the train. Dialogue (No ticket)

Ticket, please.

Fahrkarte bitte.
[fa:ɐ̯ˌkaʁtə bɪtə]

I don't have a ticket.

Ich habe keine Fahrkarte.
[ɪç 'ha:bə kaɪnə 'fa:ɐ̯ˌkaʁtə]

I lost my ticket.

Ich habe meine Fahrkarte verloren.
[ɪç 'ha:bə maɪnə 'fa:ɐ̯ˌkaʁtə fɛɐ'lo:ʁən]

I forgot my ticket at home.

Ich habe meine Fahrkarte zuhause vergessen.
[ɪç 'ha:bə maɪnə 'fa:ɐ̯ˌkaʁtə tsu'haʊzə fɛɐ'gɛsən]

You can buy a ticket from me.

Sie können von mir eine Fahrkarte kaufen.
[zi: 'kœnən fɔn mi:ɐ 'aɪnə 'fa:ɐ̯ˌkaʁtə 'kaʊfən]

You will also have to pay a fine.

Sie werden auch eine Strafe zahlen.
[zi: 've:ɐdən aʊχ 'aɪnə 'ʃtʁa:fə 'tsa:lən]

Okay.

Gut.
[gu:t]

Where are you going?

Wohin fahren Sie?
[vo'hɪn 'fa:ʁən zi:?]

I'm going to ...

Ich fahre nach ...
[ɪç 'fa:ʁə na:χ ...]

How much? I don't understand.

Wie viel? Ich verstehe nicht.
[vi: fi:l? ɪç fɛɐ'ʃte:ə nɪçt]

Write it down, please.

Schreiben Sie es bitte auf.
[ʃʁaɪbən zi: ɛs 'bɪtə aʊf]

Okay. Can I pay with a credit card?

Gut. Kann ich mit Karte zahlen?
[gu:t. kan ɪç mɪt 'kaʁtə 'tsa:lən?]

Yes, you can.

Ja, das können Sie.
[ja:, das 'kœnən zi:]

Here's your receipt.

Hier ist ihre Quittung.
[hi:ɐ ist 'i:ʁə 'kvɪtʊŋ]

Sorry about the fine.

Tut mir leid wegen der Strafe.
[tu:t mi:ɐ laɪt 've:gən de:ɐ 'ʃtʁa:fə]

That's okay. It was my fault.

Das ist in Ordnung. Es ist meine Schuld.
[das is ɪn 'ɔʁdnʊŋ. ɛs ist 'maɪnə ʃʊlt]

Enjoy your trip.

Genießen Sie Ihre Fahrt.
[gə'ni:sən zi: 'i:ʁə fa:ɐt]

Taxi

taxi
Taxi
[taksi]

taxi driver
Taxifahrer
[taksi͜fa:ʀɐ]

to catch a taxi
Ein Taxi nehmen
[aɪn 'taksi 'ne:mən]

taxi stand
Taxistand
[taksiʃtant]

Where can I get a taxi?
Wo kann ich ein Taxi bekommen?
[vo: kan ɪç aɪn 'taksi be'kɔmən?]

to call a taxi
Ein Taxi rufen
[aɪn 'taksi 'ʀu:fən]

I need a taxi.
Ich brauche ein Taxi.
[ɪç 'bʀaʊχə aɪn 'taksi]

Right now.
Jetzt sofort.
[jɛtst zo'fɔʀt]

What is your address (location)?
Wie ist Ihre Adresse?
[vi ist 'i:ʀə a'dʀɛsə?]

My address is ...
Meine Adresse ist ...
[maɪnə a'dʀɛsə ist ...]

Your destination?
Ihr Ziel?
[i:ɐ tsi:l?]

Excuse me, ...
Entschuldigen Sie bitte, ...
[ɛnt'ʃʊldɪgən zi: 'bɪtə, ...]

Are you available?
Sind Sie frei?
[zɪnt zi: fʀaɪ?]

How much is it to get to ...?
Was kostet die Fahrt nach ...?
[vas 'ko:stət di fa:ɐt naχ ...?]

Do you know where it is?
Wissen Sie wo es ist?
[vɪsən zi: vo: ɛs 'ist?]

Airport, please.
Flughafen, bitte.
[flu:k͜ha:fən, 'bɪtə]

Stop here, please.
Halten Sie hier bitte an.
[haltən zi: hi:ɐ 'bɪtə an]

It's not here.
Das ist nicht hier.
[das is nɪçt hi:ɐ]

This is the wrong address.
Das ist die falsche Adresse.
[das is di: 'falʃə a'dʀɛsə]

Turn left.
nach links
[na:χ lɪŋks]

Turn right.
nach rechts
[na:χ ʀɛçts]

How much do I owe you?	**Was schulde ich Ihnen?** [vas 'ʃʊldə ɪç 'iːnən?]
I'd like a receipt, please.	**Ich würde gerne** **ein Quittung haben, bitte.** [ɪç 'vʏʁdə 'gɛʁnə aɪn 'kvɪtʊŋ 'haːbən, 'bɪtə]
Keep the change.	**Stimmt so.** [ʃtɪmt zoː]

Would you please wait for me?	**Warten Sie auf mich bitte.** [vaʁtən ziː 'aʊf mɪç 'bɪtə]
five minutes	**fünf Minuten** [fʏnf miˈnuːtən]
ten minutes	**zehn Minuten** [tseːn miˈnuːtən]
fifteen minutes	**fünfzehn Minuten** [fʏnftseːn miˈnuːtən]
twenty minutes	**zwanzig Minuten** [tsvantsɪç miˈnuːtən]
half an hour	**eine halbe Stunde** [aɪnə 'halbə 'ʃtʊndə]

Hotel

Hello.	**Guten Tag.** [ˌɡuːtən ˈtaːk]
My name is …	**Mein Name ist …** [maɪn ˈnaːmə ist …]
I have a reservation.	**Ich habe eine Reservierung.** [ɪç ˈhaːbɛ ˈaɪnə ʁezɛʁˈviːʁʊŋ]
I need …	**Ich brauche …** [ɪç ˈbʁaʊχə …]
a single room	**ein Einzelzimmer** [aɪn ˈaɪntsəlˌtsɪmɐ]
a double room	**ein Doppelzimmer** [aɪn ˈdɔpəlˌtsɪmɐ]
How much is that?	**Wie viel kostet das?** [viː fiːl ˈkɔstət das?]
That's a bit expensive.	**Das ist ein bisschen teuer.** [das is aɪn ˈbɪsçən ˈtɔɪɐ]
Do you have anything else?	**Haben Sie sonst noch etwas?** [ˈhaːbən ziː zɔnst nɔχ ˈɛtvas?]
I'll take it.	**Ich nehme es.** [ɪç ˈneːmə ɛs]
I'll pay in cash.	**Ich zahle bar.** [ɪç ˈtsaːlə baːɐ]
I've got a problem.	**Ich habe ein Problem.** [ɪç ˈhaːbə aɪn pʁoˈbleːm]
My … is broken.	**… ist kaputt.** [… ɪst kaˈpʊt]
My … is out of order.	**… ist außer Betrieb.** [… ɪst ˈaʊsə bəˈtʁiːp]
TV	**Mein Fernseher** [maɪn ˈfɛʁnˌzeːɐ]
air conditioner	**Meine Klimaanlage** [maɪnə ˈkliːmaˌʔanlaːɡə]
tap	**Mein Wasserhahn** [maɪn ˈvasəˌhaːn]
shower	**Meine Dusche** [maɪnə ˈduːʃə]
sink	**Mein Waschbecken** [maɪn ˈvaʃˌbɛkən]
safe	**Mein Tresor** [maɪn tʁeˈzoːɐ]

door lock	**Mein Türschloss** [maɪn 'tyːʃlɔs]
electrical outlet	**Meine Steckdose** [maɪnə 'ʃtɛkˌdoːzə]
hairdryer	**Mein Föhn** [maɪn føːn]

I don't have ...	**Ich habe kein ...** [ɪç 'haːbə kaɪn ...]
water	**Wasser** [vasə]
light	**Licht** [lɪçt]
electricity	**Strom** [ʃtʀoːm]

Can you give me ...?	**Können Sie mir ... geben?** [kœnən ziː miːə ... 'geːbən?]
a towel	**ein Handtuch** [aɪn 'hantˌtuːx]
a blanket	**eine Decke** [aɪnə 'dɛkə]
slippers	**Hausschuhe** [haʊsʃuːə]
a robe	**einen Bademantel** [aɪnən 'baːdəˌmantəl]
shampoo	**etwas Shampoo** [ɛtvas 'ʃampu]
soap	**etwas Seife** [ɛtvas 'zaɪfə]

I'd like to change rooms.	**Ich möchte ein anderes Zimmer haben.** [ɪç 'mœçtə aɪn 'andəʀəs 'tsɪmə 'haːbən]
I can't find my key.	**Ich kann meinen Schlüssel nicht finden.** [ɪç kan 'maɪnən 'ʃlʏsəl nɪçt 'fɪndən]
Could you open my room, please?	**Machen Sie bitte meine Tür auf.** ['maxən ziː 'bɪtə 'maɪnə tyːə 'aʊf]

Who's there?	**Wer ist da?** [veːə ist daː?]
Come in!	**Kommen Sie rein!** [kɔmən ziː ʀaɪn!]
Just a minute!	**Einen Moment bitte!** [aɪnən moˈmɛnt 'bɪtə!]
Not right now, please.	**Nicht jetzt bitte.** [nɪçt jɛtst 'bɪtə]
Come to my room, please.	**Kommen Sie bitte in mein Zimmer.** [kɔmən ziː 'bɪtə ɪn maɪn 'tsɪmə]

I'd like to order food service.	**Ich würde gerne Essen bestellen.**
	[ɪç 'vʏʁdə 'gɛʁnə 'ɛsən bə'ʃtɛlən]
My room number is …	**Meine Zimmernummer ist …**
	[maɪnə 'tsɪmeˌnʊmə ist …]

I'm leaving …	**Ich reise … ab.**
	[ɪç 'ʁaɪzə … ap]
We're leaving …	**Wir reisen … ab.**
	[viːɐ 'ʁaɪzən … ap]
right now	**jetzt**
	[jɛtst]
this afternoon	**diesen Nachmittag**
	[diːzən 'naːxmɪˌtaːk]
tonight	**heute Abend**
	[hɔɪtə 'aːbənt]
tomorrow	**morgen**
	[mɔʁgən]
tomorrow morning	**morgen früh**
	[mɔʁgən fʁyː]
tomorrow evening	**morgen Abend**
	[mɔʁgən 'aːbənt]
the day after tomorrow	**übermorgen**
	[yːbeˌmɔʁgən]

I'd like to pay.	**Ich möchte die Zimmerrechnung begleichen.**
	[ɪç 'mœçtə di 'tsɪmeˌʁɛçnʊŋ bə'glaɪçən]
Everything was wonderful.	**Alles war wunderbar.**
	[aləs vaːɐ 'vʊndebaːɐ]
Where can I get a taxi?	**Wo kann ich ein Taxi bekommen?**
	[voː kan ɪç aɪn 'taksi be'kɔmən?]
Would you call a taxi for me, please?	**Würden Sie bitte ein Taxi für mich holen?**
	[vʏʁdən ziː 'bɪtə aɪn 'taksi fyːɐ mɪç 'hoːlən?]

Restaurant

Can I look at the menu, please?	**Könnte ich die Speisekarte sehen bitte?** [kœntə ɪç di 'ʃpaɪzə͵kaʁtə 'zeːən 'bɪtə?]
Table for one.	**Tisch für einen.** [tɪʃ fyːə 'aɪnən]
There are two (three, four) of us.	**Wir sind zu zweit (dritt, viert).** [viːə zɪnt tsu tsvaɪt (dʁɪt, fiːət)]

Smoking	**Raucher** [ʁaʊχɐ]
No smoking	**Nichtraucher** [nɪçt͵ʁaʊχɐ]
Excuse me! (addressing a waiter)	**Entschuldigen Sie mich!** [ɛntʃʊldɪgən zi: mɪç!]
menu	**Speisekarte** [ʃpaɪzə͵kaʁtə]
wine list	**Weinkarte** [vaɪn͵kaʁtə]
The menu, please.	**Die Speisekarte bitte.** [di 'ʃpaɪzə͵kaʁtə 'bɪtə]
Are you ready to order?	**Sind Sie bereit zum bestellen?** [zɪnt zi: bə'ʁaɪt tsʊm bə'ʃtɛlən?]
What will you have?	**Was würden Sie gerne haben?** [vas 'vʏʁdən zi: 'gɛʁnə 'ha:bən?]
I'll have ...	**Ich möchte ...** [ɪç 'mœçtə ...]

I'm a vegetarian.	**Ich bin Vegetarier /Vegetarierin/.** [ɪç bɪn vege'ta:ʁɪɐ /vege'ta:ʁɪəʁɪn/]
meat	**Fleisch** [flaɪʃ]
fish	**Fisch** [fɪʃ]
vegetables	**Gemüse** [gə'my:zə]
Do you have vegetarian dishes?	**Haben Sie vegetarisches Essen?** [ha:bən zi: vege'ta:ʁɪʃəs 'ɛsən?]
I don't eat pork.	**Ich esse kein Schweinefleisch.** [ɪç 'ɛsə kaɪn 'ʃvaɪnə͵flaɪʃ]
Band-Aid	**Er /Sie/ isst kein Fleisch.** [e:ɐ /zi/ ist kaɪn flaɪʃ]
I am allergic to ...	**Ich bin allergisch auf ...** [ɪç bɪn a'lɛʁgɪʃ aʊf ...]

Would you please bring me ...

Könnten Sie mir bitte ... bringen.
[kœntən zi: mi:ɐ 'bɪtə ... 'bʀɪŋən]

salt | pepper | sugar

Salz | Pfeffer | Zucker
[zalts | 'pfɛfɐ | 'tsʊkɐ]

coffee | tea | dessert

Kaffee | Tee | Nachtisch
[kafe | te: | 'na:χˌtɪʃ]

water | sparkling | plain

Wasser | Sprudel | stilles
[vasɐ | 'ʃpʀuːdəl | 'ʃtɪləs]

a spoon | fork | knife

einen Löffel | eine Gabel | ein Messer
[aɪnən 'lœfəl | 'aɪnə 'gabəl | aɪn 'mɛsɐ]

a plate | napkin

einen Teller | eine Serviette
[aɪnən 'tɛlɐ | 'aɪnə zɛʀ'vɪɛtə]

Enjoy your meal!

Guten Appetit!
[ˌgutən ˌʔapə'tit!]

One more, please.

Noch einen bitte.
[nɔχ 'aɪnən 'bɪtə]

It was very delicious.

Es war sehr lecker.
[ɛs vaːɐ zeːɐ 'lɛkɐ]

---

check | change | tip

Scheck | Wechselgeld | Trinkgeld
[ʃɛk | 'vɛksəlˌgɛlt | 'tʀɪŋkˌgɛlt]

Check, please.
(Could I have the check, please?)

Zahlen bitte.
[tsaːlən 'bɪtə]

Can I pay by credit card?

Kann ich mit Karte zahlen?
[kan ɪç mɪt 'kaʀtə 'tsaːlən?]

I'm sorry, there's a mistake here.

Entschuldigen Sie, hier ist ein Fehler.
[ɛnt'ʃʊldɪgən ziː, hiːɐ ist aɪn 'feːlɐ]

Shopping

Can I help you?
Kann ich Ihnen behilflich sein?
[kan ɪç 'iːnən bə'hɪlflɪç zaɪn?]

Do you have ...?
Haben Sie ...?
[haːbən ziː ...?]

I'm looking for ...
Ich suche ...
[ɪç 'zuːχə ...]

I need ...
Ich brauche ...
[ɪç 'bʀaʊχə ...]

I'm just looking.
Ich möchte nur schauen.
[ɪç 'mœçtə nuːə 'ʃaʊən]

We're just looking.
Wir möchten nur schauen.
[viːɐ 'mœçtən nuːɐ 'ʃaʊən]

I'll come back later.
Ich komme später noch einmal zurück.
[ɪç 'kɔmə 'ʃpɛːtə nɔχ 'aɪnmaːl tsuˈʀʏk]

We'll come back later.
Wir kommen später vorbei.
[viːɐ 'kɔmən 'ʃpɛːtə foːɐ'baɪ]

discounts | sale
Rabatt | Ausverkauf
[ʀa'bat | 'aʊsfɛɐˌkaʊf]

Would you please show me ...
Zeigen Sie mir bitte ...
[tsaɪgən ziː miːɐ 'bɪtə ...]

Would you please give me ...
Geben Sie mir bitte ...
[geːbən ziː miːɐ 'bɪtə ...]

Can I try it on?
Kann ich es anprobieren?
[kan ɪç ɛs 'anpʀoˌbiːʀən?]

Excuse me, where's the fitting room?
Entschuldigen Sie bitte, wo ist die Anprobe?
[ɛnt'ʃʊldɪgən ziː 'bɪtə, voː ist di 'anpʀoːbə?]

Which color would you like?
Welche Farbe mögen Sie?
[vɛlçə 'faʀbə 'møgən ziː?]

size | length
Größe | Länge
[gʀøːsə | 'lɛŋə]

How does it fit?
Wie sitzt es?
[viː zɪtst ɛs?]

How much is it?
Was kostet das?
[vas 'koːstət das?]

That's too expensive.
Das ist zu teuer.
[das is tsu 'tɔɪɐ]

I'll take it.

Ich nehme es.
[ɪç 'neːmə ɛs]

Excuse me, where do I pay?

Entschuldigen Sie bitte,
wo ist die Kasse?
[ɛnt'ʃʊldɪgən ziː 'bɪtə,
voː ist diː 'kasə?]

Will you pay in cash or credit card?

Zahlen Sie Bar oder mit Karte?
[tsaːlən ziː baːɐ 'oːdɐ mɪt 'kaʁtə?]

In cash | with credit card

in Bar | mit Karte
[ɪn baːɐ | mɪt 'kaʁtə]

Do you want the receipt?

Brauchen Sie die Quittung?
[bʁaʊχən ziː diː 'kvɪtʊŋ?]

Yes, please.

Ja, bitte.
[jaː, 'bɪtə]

No, it's OK.

Nein, es ist ok.
[naɪn, ɛs ist o'keː]

Thank you. Have a nice day!

Danke. Einen schönen Tag noch!
[daŋkə. 'aɪnən 'ʃøːnən 'tak nɔχ!]

In town

Excuse me, ...	**Entschuldigen Sie bitte, ...** [ɛnt'ʃuldɪgən ziː 'bɪtə, ...]
I'm looking for ...	**Ich suche ...** [ɪç 'zuːχə ...]
the subway	**die U-Bahn** [di 'uːbaːn]
my hotel	**mein Hotel** [maɪn ho'tɛl]
the movie theater	**das Kino** [das 'kiːno]
a taxi stand	**den Taxistand** [den 'taksiʃtant]

an ATM	**einen Geldautomat** [aɪnən 'gɛlt?autoˌmaːt]
a foreign exchange office	**eine Wechselstube** [aɪnə 'vɛksəlʃtuːbə]
an internet café	**ein Internetcafé** [aɪn 'ɪntənɛt·kaˌfeː]
... street	**die ... -Straße** [di ... 'ʃtʀaːsə]
this place	**diesen Ort** [diːzən ɔʀt]

Do you know where ... is?	**Wissen Sie, wo ... ist?** [vɪsən ziː, voː ... 'ist?]
Which street is this?	**Wie heißt diese Straße?** [viː haɪst 'diːzə 'ʃtʀaːsə?]
Show me where we are right now.	**Zeigen Sie mir wo wir gerade sind.** [tsaɪgən ziː miːɐ voː viːɐ gəˈʀaːdə zɪnt]
Can I get there on foot?	**Kann ich dort zu Fuß hingehen?** [kan ɪç dɔʀt tsu fuːs 'hɪnˌgeːən?]
Do you have a map of the city?	**Haben Sie einen Stadtplan?** [haːbən ziː 'aɪnən 'ʃtatˌplaːn?]

How much is a ticket to get in?	**Was kostet eine Eintrittskarte?** [vas 'koːstət 'aɪnə 'aɪntʀɪtsˌkaʀtə?]
Can I take pictures here?	**Darf man hier fotografieren?** [daʀf man hiːɐ fotogʀaˈfiːʀən?]
Are you open?	**Haben Sie offen?** [haːbən ziː 'ɔfən?]

When do you open? **Wann öffnen Sie?**
[van 'œfnən zi:?]

When do you close? **Wann schließen Sie?**
[van 'ʃli:sən zi:?]

Money

money	**Geld** [gɛlt]
cash	**Bargeld** [baːɐˌgɛlt]
paper money	**Papiergeld** [pa'piːɐˌgɛlt]
loose change	**Kleingeld** [klaɪŋˌgɛlt]
check | change | tip	**Scheck | Wechselgeld | Trinkgeld** [ʃɛk | 'vɛksəlˌgɛlt | 'tʀɪŋkˌgɛlt]
credit card	**Kreditkarte** [kʀe'diːtˌkaʀtə]
wallet	**Geldbeutel** [gɛltˌbɔɪtəl]
to buy	**kaufen** [kaʊfən]
to pay	**zahlen** [tsaːlən]
fine	**Strafe** [ʃtʀaːfə]
free	**kostenlos** [kɔstənloːs]
Where can I buy ...?	**Wo kann ich ... kaufen?** [voː kan ɪç ... 'kaʊfən?]
Is the bank open now?	**Ist die Bank jetzt offen?** [ist di baŋk jɛtst 'ɔfən?]
When does it open?	**Wann öffnet sie?** [van 'œfnət ziː?]
When does it close?	**Wann schließt sie?** [van ʃliːst ziː?]
How much?	**Wie viel?** [viː fiːl?]
How much is this?	**Was kostet das?** [vas 'koːstət das?]
That's too expensive.	**Das ist zu teuer.** [das is tsu 'tɔɪɐ]
Excuse me, where do I pay?	**Entschuldigen Sie bitte, wo ist die Kasse?** [ɛnt'ʃʊldɪgən ziː 'bɪtə, voː ist di 'kasə?]

Check, please.

Ich möchte zahlen.
[ɪç 'mœçtə 'tsaːlən]

Can I pay by credit card?

Kann ich mit Karte zahlen?
[kan ɪç mɪt 'kaʁtə 'tsaːlən?]

Is there an ATM here?

Gibt es hier einen Geldautomat?
[giːpt ɛs hiːɐ 'aɪnən 'gɛltʔautoˌmaːt?]

I'm looking for an ATM.

Ich brauche einen Geldautomat.
[ɪç 'bʁauxə 'aɪnən 'gɛltʔautoˌmaːt]

I'm looking for a foreign exchange
office.

Ich suche eine Wechselstube.
[ɪç 'zuːxə 'aɪnə 'vɛksəlˌʃtuːbə]

I'd like to change ...

Ich möchte ... wechseln.
[ɪç 'mœçtə ... 'vɛksəln]

What is the exchange rate?

Was ist der Wechselkurs?
[vas ɪst deːɐ 'vɛksəlˌkuʁs]

Do you need my passport?

Brauchen Sie meinen Reisepass?
[bʁauxən ziː 'maɪnən 'ʁaɪzəˌpas?]

Time

What time is it?	**Wie spät ist es?** [vi: ʃpɛ:t ist ɛs?]
When?	**Wann?** [van?]
At what time?	**Um wie viel Uhr?** [ʊm vifi:l u:ɐ?]
now | later | after …	**jetzt | später | nach …** [jɛtst | 'ʃpɛ:tɐ | na:χ …]
one o'clock	**ein Uhr** [aɪn u:ɐ]
one fifteen	**Viertel zwei** [fɪʁtəl tsvaɪ]
one thirty	**ein Uhr dreißig** [aɪn u:ɐ 'dʁaɪsɪç]
one forty-five	**Viertel vor zwei** [fɪʁtəl fo:ɐ tsvaɪ]
one | two | three	**eins | zwei | drei** [aɪns | tsvaɪ | dʁaɪ]
four | five | six	**vier | fünf | sechs** [fi:ɐ | fʏnf | zɛks]
seven | eight | nine	**sieben | acht | neun** [zi:bən | aχt | nɔɪn]
ten | eleven | twelve	**zehn | elf | zwölf** [tse:n | ɛlf | tsvœlf]
in …	**in …** [ɪn …]
five minutes	**fünf Minuten** [fʏnf mi'nu:tən]
ten minutes	**zehn Minuten** [tse:n mi'nu:tən]
fifteen minutes	**fünfzehn Minuten** [fʏnftse:n mi'nu:tən]
twenty minutes	**zwanzig Minuten** [tsvantsɪç mi'nu:tən]
half an hour	**einer halben Stunde** [aɪnɐ 'halbən 'ʃtʊndə]
an hour	**einer Stunde** [aɪnɐ 'ʃtʊndə]

in the morning

am Vormittag
[am 'fo:ɐmɪta:k]

early in the morning

früh am Morgen
[fʀy: am 'mɔʁgən]

this morning

diesen Morgen
[di:zən 'mɔʁgən]

tomorrow morning

morgen früh
[mɔʁgən fʀy:]

in the middle of the day

am Mittag
[am 'mɪta:k]

in the afternoon

am Nachmittag
[am 'na:χmɪta:k]

in the evening

am Abend
[am 'a:bənt]

tonight

heute Abend
[hɔɪtə 'a:bənt]

at night

in der Nacht
[ɪn de:ɐ naχt]

yesterday

gestern
[gɛsten]

today

heute
[hɔɪtə]

tomorrow

morgen
[mɔʁgən]

the day after tomorrow

übermorgen
[y:bɐˌmɔʁgən]

What day is it today?

Welcher Tag ist heute?
[vɛlçɐ ta:k ist 'hɔɪtə?]

It's ...

Es ist ...
[ɛs ist ...]

Monday

Montag
[mo:nta:k]

Tuesday

Dienstag
[di:nsta:k]

Wednesday

Mittwoch
[mɪtvɔχ]

Thursday

Donnerstag
[dɔnɛsta:k]

Friday

Freitag
[fʀaɪta:k]

Saturday

Samstag
[zamsta:k]

Sunday

Sonntag
[zɔnta:k]

Greetings. Introductions

Hello.

Hallo.
[ha'lo:]

Pleased to meet you.

Freut mich, Sie kennen zu lernen.
[fʀɔɪt mɪç, zi: 'kɛnən tsu 'lɛʀnən]

Me too.

Ganz meinerseits.
[gants 'maɪnəˌzaɪts]

I'd like you to meet ...

Darf ich vorstellen? Das ist ...
[daʀf ɪç 'fo:ɐˌʃtɛlən? das ɪs ...]

Nice to meet you.

Sehr angenehm.
[ze:ɐ 'angəˌne:m]

How are you?

Wie geht es Ihnen?
[vi: ge:t ɛs 'i:nən?]

My name is ...

Ich heiße ...
[ɪç 'haɪsə ...]

His name is ...

Er heißt ...
[e:ɐ haɪst ...]

Her name is ...

Sie heißt ...
[zi: haɪst ...]

What's your name?

Wie heißen Sie?
[vi: 'haɪsən zi:?]

What's his name?

Wie heißt er?
[vi: haɪst e:ɐ?]

What's her name?

Wie heißt sie?
[vi: haɪst zi:?]

What's your last name?

Wie ist Ihr Nachname?
[vi: ist i:ɐ 'na:χˌna:mə?]

You can call me ...

Sie können mich ... nennen.
[zi: 'kœnən mɪç ... 'nɛnən]

Where are you from?

Woher kommen Sie?
[vo'he:ɐ 'kɔmən zi:?]

I'm from ...

Ich komme aus ...
[ɪç 'kɔmə 'aʊs ...]

What do you do for a living?

Was machen Sie beruflich?
[vas 'maχən zi: bə'ʀu:flɪç?]

Who is this?

Wer ist das?
[ve:ɐ ist das?]

Who is he?

Wer ist er?
[ve:ɐ ist e:ɐ?]

Who is she?

Wer ist sie?
[ve:ɐ ist zi:?]

Who are they?

Wer sind sie?
[ve:ɐ zɪnt zi:?]

This is ...
Das ist ...
[das is ...]

my friend (masc.)
mein Freund
[maɪn fʀɔɪnt]

my friend (fem.)
meine Freundin
[maɪnə 'fʀɔɪndin]

my husband
mein Mann
[maɪn man]

my wife
meine Frau
[maɪnə 'fʀaʊ]

my father
mein Vater
[maɪn 'fa:tə]

my mother
meine Mutter
[maɪnə 'mʊtə]

my brother
mein Bruder
[maɪn 'bʀu:də]

my sister
meine Schwester
[maɪnə 'ʃvɛstə]

my son
mein Sohn
[maɪn zo:n]

my daughter
meine Tochter
[maɪnə 'tɔχtə]

This is our son.
Das ist unser Sohn.
[das is 'ʊnzə zo:n]

This is our daughter.
Das ist unsere Tochter.
[das is 'ʊnzəʀə 'tɔχtə]

These are my children.
Das sind meine Kinder.
[das zɪnt 'maɪnə 'kɪndə]

These are our children.
Das sind unsere Kinder.
[das zɪnt 'ʊnzəʀə 'kɪndə]

Farewells

Good bye!	**Auf Wiedersehen!** [aʊf 'viːdəˌzeːən!]
Bye! (inform.)	**Tschüs!** [tʃyːs!]
See you tomorrow.	**Bis morgen.** [bɪs 'mɔʁgən]
See you soon.	**Bis bald.** [bɪs balt]
See you at seven.	**Bis um sieben.** [bɪs ʊm ziːbən]
Have fun!	**Viel Spaß!** [fiːl ʃpaːs!]
Talk to you later.	**Wir sprechen später.** [viːɐ 'ʃpʁɛçən 'ʃpɛːtə]
Have a nice weekend.	**Ich wünsche Ihnen ein schönes Wochenende.** [ɪç 'vʏnʃə 'iːnən aɪn 'ʃøːnəs 'vɔχənˌʔɛndə]
Good night.	**Gute Nacht.** [guːtə naχt]
It's time for me to go.	**Es ist Zeit, dass ich gehe.** [ɛs ist tsaɪt, das ɪç 'geːə]
I have to go.	**Ich muss gehen.** [ɪç mʊs 'geːən]
I will be right back.	**Ich bin gleich wieder da.** [ɪç bɪn glaɪç 'viːdə da]
It's late.	**Es ist schon spät.** [ɛs ist ʃoːn ʃpɛːt]
I have to get up early.	**Ich muss früh aufstehen.** [ɪç mʊs fʁyː 'aʊfˌʃteːən]
I'm leaving tomorrow.	**Ich reise morgen ab.** [ɪç 'ʁaɪzə 'mɔʁgən ap]
We're leaving tomorrow.	**Wir reisen morgen ab.** [viːɐ 'ʁaɪzən 'mɔʁgən ap]
Have a nice trip!	**Ich wünsche Ihnen eine gute Reise!** [ɪç 'vʏnʃə 'iːnən 'aɪnə 'guːtə 'ʁaɪzə!]
It was nice meeting you.	**Hat mich gefreut, Sie kennen zu lernen.** [hat mɪç gə'fʁɔɪt, ziː 'kɛnən tsu 'lɛʁnən]

It was nice talking to you.

Hat mich gefreut mit Ihnen zu sprechen.
[hat mɪç gə'frɔɪt mɪt 'i:nən tsu 'ʃprɛçən]

Thanks for everything.

Danke für alles.
[daŋkə fy:ɐ 'aləs]

I had a very good time.

Ich hatte eine sehr gute Zeit.
[ɪç hatə 'aɪnə ze:ɐ 'gu:tə tsaɪt]

We had a very good time.

Wir hatten eine sehr gute Zeit.
[vi:ɐ 'hatən 'aɪnə ze:ɐ 'gu:tə tsaɪt]

It was really great.

Es war wirklich toll.
[ɛs va:ɐ 'vɪʁklɪç tɔl]

I'm going to miss you.

Ich werde Sie vermissen.
[ɪç 've:ɐdə zi: fɛɐ'mɪsən]

We're going to miss you.

Wir werden Sie vermissen.
[vi:ɐ 've:ɐdən zi: fɛɐ'mɪsən]

Good luck!

Viel Glück!
[fi:l glʏk!]

Say hi to ...

Grüßen Sie ...
[gʁy:sən zi: ...]

Foreign language

I don't understand.	**Ich verstehe nicht.** [ɪç fɛɐ'ʃteːə nɪçt]
Write it down, please.	**Schreiben Sie es bitte auf.** [ʃʀaɪbən ziː ɛs 'bɪtə aʊf]
Do you speak ...?	**Sprechen Sie ...?** [ʃpʀɛçən ziː ...?]

I speak a little bit of ...	**Ich spreche ein bisschen ...** [ɪç 'ʃpʀɛçə aɪn 'bɪsçən ...]
English	**Englisch** [ɛŋlɪʃ]
Turkish	**Türkisch** [tʏʁkɪʃ]
Arabic	**Arabisch** [a'ʀaːbɪʃ]
French	**Französisch** [fʀan'tsøːzɪʃ]

German	**Deutsch** [dɔɪtʃ]
Italian	**Italienisch** [ˌita'lɪeːnɪʃ]
Spanish	**Spanisch** [ʃpaːnɪʃ]
Portuguese	**Portugiesisch** [pɔʁtu'giːzɪʃ]
Chinese	**Chinesisch** [çi'neːzɪʃ]
Japanese	**Japanisch** [ja'paːnɪʃ]

Can you repeat that, please.	**Können Sie das bitte wiederholen.** [kœnən ziː das 'bɪtə viːdɐ'hoːlən]
I understand.	**Ich verstehe.** [ɪç fɛɐ'ʃteːə]
I don't understand.	**Ich verstehe nicht.** [ɪç fɛɐ'ʃteːə nɪçt]
Please speak more slowly.	**Sprechen Sie etwas langsamer.** [ʃpʀɛçən ziː 'ɛtvas 'laŋˌzaːmɐ]

Is that correct? (Am I saying it right?)	**Ist das richtig?** [ist das 'ʀɪçtɪç?]
What is this? (What does this mean?)	**Was ist das?** [vas ɪst das?]

Apologies

Excuse me, please.

Entschuldigen Sie bitte.
[ɛnt'ʃʊldɪgən zi: 'bɪtə]

I'm sorry.

Es tut mir leid.
[ɛs tu:t mi:ɐ laɪt]

I'm really sorry.

Es tut mir sehr leid.
[ɛs tu:t mi:ɐ ze:ɐ laɪt]

Sorry, it's my fault.

Es tut mir leid, das ist meine Schuld.
[ɛs tu:t mi:ɐ laɪt, das ist 'maɪnə ʃʊlt]

My mistake.

Das ist mein Fehler.
[das is maɪn 'fe:lɐ]

May I ...?

Darf ich ...?
[daʁf ɪç ...?]

Do you mind if I ...?

**Haben Sie etwas dagegen,
wenn ich ...?**
[ha:bən zi: 'ɛtvas da'ge:gən,
vɛn ɪç ...?]

It's OK.

Es ist okay.
[ɛs ist o'ke:]

It's all right.

Alles in Ordnung.
[aləs ɪn 'ɔʁdnʊŋ]

Don't worry about it.

Machen Sie sich keine Sorgen.
['maxən zi: zɪç 'kaɪnə 'zɔʁgən]

Agreement

Yes.	**Ja.** [ja:]
Yes, sure.	**Ja, natürlich.** [ja:, na'ty:ɐlɪç]
OK (Good!)	**Ok! Gut!** [o'ke:! gu:t!]
Very well.	**Sehr gut.** [ze:ɐ gu:t]
Certainly!	**Natürlich!** [na'ty:ɐlɪç!]
I agree.	**Genau.** [ge'naʊ]

That's correct.	**Das stimmt.** [das ʃtɪmt]
That's right.	**Das ist richtig.** [das is 'ʁɪçtɪç]
You're right.	**Sie haben Recht.** [zi: 'ha:bən ʁɛçt]
I don't mind.	**Ich habe nichts dagegen.** [ɪç 'ha:bə nɪçts da'ge:gən]
Absolutely right.	**Völlig richtig.** [fœlɪç 'ʁɪçtɪç]

It's possible.	**Das kann sein.** [das kan zaɪn]
That's a good idea.	**Das ist eine gute Idee.** [das is 'aɪnə 'gu:tə i'de:]
I can't say no.	**Ich kann es nicht ablehnen.** [ɪç kan ɛs nɪçt 'apˌle:nən]
I'd be happy to.	**Ich würde mich freuen.** [ɪç 'vʏʁdə mɪç 'fʁɔɪən]
With pleasure.	**Gerne.** [gɛʁnə]

Refusal. Expressing doubt

No.	**Nein.** [naɪn]
Certainly not.	**Natürlich nicht.** [na'ty:ɐlɪç nɪçt]
I don't agree.	**Ich stimme nicht zu.** [ɪç 'ʃtɪmə nɪçt tsu]
I don't think so.	**Das glaube ich nicht.** [das 'glaʊbə ɪç nɪçt]
It's not true.	**Das ist falsch.** [das is falʃ]
You are wrong.	**Sie liegen falsch.** [zi: 'li:gən falʃ]
I think you are wrong.	**Ich glaube, Sie haben Unrecht.** [ɪç 'glaʊbə, zi: 'ha:bən 'ʊn͵ʀɛçt]
I'm not sure.	**Ich bin nicht sicher.** [ɪç bɪn nɪçt 'zɪçɐ]
It's impossible.	**Das ist unmöglich.** [das is 'ʊnmø:klɪç]
Nothing of the kind (sort)!	**Nichts dergleichen!** [nɪçts de:ɐ'glaɪçən!]
The exact opposite.	**Im Gegenteil!** [ɪm 'ge:gəntaɪl!]
I'm against it.	**Ich bin dagegen.** [ɪç bɪn da'ge:gən]
I don't care.	**Es ist mir egal.** [ɛs ist mi:ɐ e'ga:l]
I have no idea.	**Keine Ahnung.** [kaɪnə 'a:nʊŋ]
I doubt it.	**Ich bezweifle, dass es so ist.** [ɪç bə'tsvaɪflə, das ɛs zo: ist]
Sorry, I can't.	**Es tut mir leid, ich kann nicht.** [ɛs tu:t mi:ɐ laɪt, ɪç kan nɪçt]
Sorry, I don't want to.	**Es tut mir leid, ich möchte nicht.** [ɛs tu:t mi:ɐ laɪt, ɪç 'mœçtə nɪçt]
Thank you, but I don't need this.	**Danke, das brauche ich nicht.** [daŋkə, das 'bʀaʊχə ɪç nɪçt]
It's getting late.	**Es ist schon spät.** [ɛs ist ʃo:n ʃpɛ:t]

I have to get up early.

Ich muss früh aufstehen.
[ɪç mʊs fʀy: 'aʊfʃteːən]

I don't feel well.

Mir geht es schlecht.
[miːɐ geːt ɛs ʃlɛçt]

Expressing gratitude

Thank you.
Danke.
[daŋkə]

Thank you very much.
Dankeschön.
[daŋkəʃøːn]

I really appreciate it.
Ich bin Ihnen sehr verbunden.
[ɪç bɪn 'iːnən zeːɐ ˌfɛɐ'bʊndən]

I'm really grateful to you.
Ich bin Ihnen sehr dankbar.
[ɪç bɪn 'iːnən zeːɐ 'daŋkbaːɐ]

We are really grateful to you.
Wir sind Ihnen sehr dankbar.
[viːɐ zɪnt 'iːnən zeːɐ 'daŋkbaːɐ]

Thank you for your time.
Danke, dass Sie Ihre Zeit geopfert haben.
[daŋkə, das ziː 'iːʀə tsaɪt gə'ʔɔpfet 'haːbən]

Thanks for everything.
Danke für alles.
[daŋkə fyːɐ 'aləs]

Thank you for ...
Danke für ...
[daŋkə fyːɐ ...]

your help
Ihre Hilfe
[iːʀə 'hɪlfə]

a nice time
die schöne Zeit
[di 'ʃøːnə tsaɪt]

a wonderful meal
das wunderbare Essen
[das 'vʊndɐbaːʀə 'ɛsən]

a pleasant evening
den angenehmen Abend
[den 'angəˌneːmən 'aːbənt]

a wonderful day
den wunderschönen Tag
[dɛn ˌvʊndɐ'ʃøːnən taːk]

an amazing journey
die interessante Führung
[di ɪntəʀɛ'santə 'fyːʀʊŋ]

Don't mention it.
Keine Ursache.
[kaɪnə 'uːɐˌzaχə]

You are welcome.
Nichts zu danken.
[nɪçts tsu 'daŋkən]

Any time.
Immer gerne.
[ɪmɐ 'gɛʁnə]

My pleasure.
Es freut mich, geholfen zu haben.
[ɛs fʀɔɪt mɪç, gə'hɔlfən tsu 'haːbən]

Forget it.   **Vergessen Sie es.**
                                        [fɛɐ'gɛsən ziː ɛs]

Don't worry about it.   **Machen Sie sich keine Sorgen.**
                                        ['maχən ziː zɪç 'kaɪnə 'zɔʁgən]

Congratulations. Best wishes

Congratulations!
Glückwunsch!
[glʏkˌvʊnʃ!]

Happy birthday!
Alles gute zum Geburtstag!
[aləs 'guːtə tsʊm gə'bʊʁtsˌtaːk!]

Merry Christmas!
Frohe Weihnachten!
[ˌfʁoːə 'vaɪnaxtən!]

Happy New Year!
Frohes neues Jahr!
[ˌfʁoːəs 'nɔɪəs jaːɐ̯!]

Happy Easter!
Frohe Ostern!
[ˌfʁoːə 'oːstən!]

Happy Hanukkah!
Frohes Hanukkah!
[ˌfʁoːəs 'haːnukaː!]

I'd like to propose a toast.
Ich möchte einen Toast ausbringen.
[ɪç 'mœçtə 'aɪnən toːst 'aʊsˌbʁɪŋən]

Cheers!
Auf Ihr Wohl!
[aʊf iːɐ̯ voːl!]

Let's drink to …!
Trinken wir auf …!
[tʁɪŋkən viːɐ̯ 'aʊf …!]

To our success!
Auf unseren Erfolg!
[aʊf 'ʊnzərən ɛɐ̯'fɔlk!]

To your success!
Auf Ihren Erfolg!
[aʊf 'iːʁən ɛɐ̯'fɔlk!]

Good luck!
Viel Glück!
[fiːl glʏk!]

Have a nice day!
Einen schönen Tag noch!
[aɪnən 'ʃøːnən taːk nɔx!]

Have a good holiday!
Haben Sie einen guten Urlaub!
[haːbən ziː 'aɪnən 'guːtən 'uːɐ̯ˌlaʊp!]

Have a safe journey!
Haben Sie eine sichere Reise!
[haːbən ziː 'aɪnə 'zɪçəʁə 'ʁaɪzə!]

I hope you get better soon!
Ich hoffe es geht Ihnen bald besser!
[ɪç 'hɔfə ɛs geːt 'iːnən balt 'bɛsə!]

Socializing

Why are you sad?	**Warum sind Sie traurig?** [vaˈʀʊm zɪnt ziː ˈtʀaʊʀɪç?]
Smile! Cheer up!	**Lächeln Sie!** [lɛçəln ziː!]
Are you free tonight?	**Sind Sie heute Abend frei?** [zɪnt ziː ˈhɔɪtə ˈaːbənt fʀaɪ?]

May I offer you a drink?	**Darf ich ihnen was zum Trinken anbieten?** [daʁf ɪç ˈiːnən vas tsʊm ˈtʀɪŋkən ˈanˌbiːtən?]
Would you like to dance?	**Möchten Sie tanzen?** [mœçtən ziː ˈtantsən?]
Let's go to the movies.	**Gehen wir ins Kino.** [geːən viːɐ ɪns ˈkiːno]

May I invite you to ...?	**Darf ich Sie ins ... einladen?** [daʁf ɪç ziː ɪns ... ˈaɪnˌlaːdən?]
a restaurant	**Restaurant** [ʀɛstoˈʀaŋ]
the movies	**Kino** [kiːno]
the theater	**Theater** [teˈaːtɐ]
go for a walk	**auf einen Spaziergang** [aʊf ˈaɪnən ʃpaˈtsiːɐˌgaŋ]

At what time?	**Um wie viel Uhr?** [ʊm vifiːl uːɐ?]
tonight	**heute Abend** [hɔɪtə ˈaːbənt]
at six	**um sechs Uhr** [ʊm zɛks uːɐ]
at seven	**um sieben Uhr** [ʊm ˈziːbən uːɐ]
at eight	**um acht Uhr** [ʊm aχt uːɐ]
at nine	**um neun Uhr** [ʊm ˈnɔɪn uːɐ]

Do you like it here?	**Gefällt es Ihnen hier?** [gəˈfɛlt ɛs ˈiːnən hiːɐ?]
Are you here with someone?	**Sind Sie hier mit jemandem?** [zɪnt ziː hiːɐ mɪt ˈjeːmandəm?]

I'm with my friend.

Ich bin mit meinem Freund.
[ɪç bɪn mɪt 'maɪnəm frɔɪnt]

I'm with my friends.

Ich bin mit meinen Freunden.
[ɪç bɪn mɪt 'maɪnəm 'frɔɪndən]

No, I'm alone.

Nein, ich bin alleine.
[naɪn, ɪç bɪn a'laɪnə]

Do you have a boyfriend?

Hast du einen Freund?
[hast du 'aɪnən frɔɪnt?]

I have a boyfriend.

Ich habe einen Freund.
[ɪç 'ha:bə 'aɪnən frɔɪnt]

Do you have a girlfriend?

Hast du eine Freundin?
[hast du 'aɪnə 'frɔɪndɪn?]

I have a girlfriend.

Ich habe eine Freundin.
[ɪç 'ha:bə 'aɪnə 'frɔɪndɪn]

Can I see you again?

Kann ich dich nochmals sehen?
[kan ɪç dɪç 'nɔxma:ls 'ze:ən?]

Can I call you?

Kann ich dich anrufen?
[kan ɪç dɪç 'anˌru:fən?]

Call me. (Give me a call.)

Ruf mich an.
[ru:f mɪç an]

What's your number?

Was ist deine Nummer?
[vas ɪst 'daɪnə 'nʊmɐ?]

I miss you.

Ich vermisse dich.
[ɪç fɛɐ'mɪsə dɪç]

You have a beautiful name.

Sie haben einen schönen Namen.
[zi: 'ha:bən 'aɪnən 'ʃø:nən 'na:mən]

I love you.

Ich liebe dich.
[ɪç 'li:bə dɪç]

Will you marry me?

Willst du mich heiraten?
[vɪlst du mɪç 'haɪra:tən?]

You're kidding!

Sie machen Scherze!
[zi: 'maxən 'ʃɛɐtsə!]

I'm just kidding.

Ich habe nur gescherzt.
[ɪç 'ha:bə nu:ɐ gə'ʃɛɐtst]

Are you serious?

Ist das Ihr Ernst?
[ist das i:ɐ ɛʁnst?]

I'm serious.

Das ist mein Ernst.
[das is maɪn ɛʁnst]

Really?!

Echt?!
[ɛçt?!]

It's unbelievable!

Das ist unglaublich!
[das is ʊn'glaʊplɪç!]

I don't believe you.

Ich glaube Ihnen nicht.
[ɪç 'glaʊbə 'i:nən nɪçt]

I can't.

Ich kann nicht.
[ɪç kan nɪçt]

I don't know.

Ich weiß nicht.
[ɪç vaɪs nɪçt]

I don't understand you.	**Ich verstehe Sie nicht.** [ɪç fɛɛ'ʃteːə ziː nɪçt]
Please go away.	**Bitte gehen Sie weg.** [bɪtə 'geːən ziː vɛk]
Leave me alone!	**Lassen Sie mich in Ruhe!** [lasən ziː mɪç ɪn 'ʀuːə!]

I can't stand him.	**Ich kann ihn nicht ausstehen.** [ɪç kan iːn nɪçt 'aʊsˌʃteːən]
You are disgusting!	**Sie sind widerlich!** [ziː zɪnt 'viːdelɪç!]
I'll call the police!	**Ich rufe die Polizei an!** [ɪç 'ʀuːfə diː ˌpoliˈtsaɪ an!]

Sharing impressions. Emotions

I like it.	**Das gefällt mir.** [das gə'fɛlt miːɐ]
Very nice.	**Sehr nett.** [zeːɐ nɛt]
That's great!	**Das ist toll!** [das is tɔl!]
It's not bad.	**Das ist nicht schlecht.** [das is nɪçt ʃlɛçt]

I don't like it.	**Das gefällt mir nicht.** [das gə'fɛlt miːɐ nɪçt]
It's not good.	**Das ist nicht gut.** [das is nɪçt guːt]
It's bad.	**Das ist schlecht.** [das is ʃlɛçt]
It's very bad.	**Das ist sehr schlecht.** [das is zeːɐ ʃlɛçt]
It's disgusting.	**Das ist widerlich.** [das is 'viːdəlɪç]

I'm happy.	**Ich bin glücklich.** [ɪç bɪn 'glʏklɪç]
I'm content.	**Ich bin zufrieden.** [ɪç bɪn tsu'fʀiːdən]
I'm in love.	**Ich bin verliebt.** [ɪç bɪn fɛɐ'liːpt]
I'm calm.	**Ich bin ruhig.** [ɪç bɪn 'ʀuːɪç]
I'm bored.	**Ich bin gelangweilt.** [ɪç bɪn gə'laŋˌvaɪlt]

I'm tired.	**Ich bin müde.** [ɪç bɪn 'myːdə]
I'm sad.	**Ich bin traurig.** [ɪç bɪn 'tʀaʊʀɪç]

I'm frightened.	**Ich habe Angst.** [ɪç 'haːbə aŋst]
I'm angry.	**Ich bin wütend.** [ɪç bɪn 'vyːtənt]
I'm worried.	**Ich mache mir Sorgen.** [ɪç 'maxə miːɐ 'zɔʀgən]
I'm nervous.	**Ich bin nervös.** [ɪç bɪn nɛʀ'vøːs]

I'm jealous. (envious)

Ich bin eifersüchtig.
[ɪç bɪn 'aɪfɐˌzʏçtɪç]

I'm surprised.

Ich bin überrascht.
[ɪç bɪn y:bɐ'ʀaʃt]

I'm perplexed.

Es ist mir peinlich.
[ɛs ist mi:ɐ 'paɪnˌlɪç]

Problems. Accidents

I've got a problem.	**Ich habe ein Problem.** [ɪç 'haːbə aɪn pʀoˈbleːm]
We've got a problem.	**Wir haben Probleme.** [viːɐ 'haːbən pʀoˈbleːmə]
I'm lost.	**Ich bin verloren.** [ɪç bɪn fɛɐˈloːʀən]
I missed the last bus (train).	**Ich habe den letzten Bus (Zug) verpasst.** [ɪç 'haːbə den 'lɛtstən bʊs (tsuːk) fɛɐˈpast]
I don't have any money left.	**Ich habe kein Geld mehr.** [ɪç 'haːbə kaɪn gɛlt meːɐ]
I've lost my ...	**Ich habe mein ... verloren.** [ɪç 'haːbə maɪn ... fɛɐˈloːʀən]
Someone stole my ...	**Jemand hat mein ... gestohlen.** [jeːmant hat maɪn ... gəˈʃtoːlən]
passport	**Reisepass** [ʀaɪzəˌpas]
wallet	**Geldbeutel** [gɛltˌbɔɪtəl]
papers	**Papiere** [paˈpiːʀə]
ticket	**Fahrkarte** [faːɐˌkaʀtə]
money	**Geld** [gɛlt]
handbag	**Tasche** [taʃə]
camera	**Kamera** [kaməʀa]
laptop	**Laptop** [lɛptɔp]
tablet computer	**Tabletcomputer** [tɛblət·kɔmˌpjuːtɐ]
mobile phone	**Handy** [hɛndi]
Help me!	**Hilfe!** [hɪlfə!]
What's happened?	**Was ist passiert?** [vas ɪst paˈsiːɐt?]
fire	**Feuer** [fɔɪɐ]

shooting	**Schießerei** [ˈʃiːsəˈʀaɪ]
murder	**Mord** [mɔʁt]
explosion	**Explosion** [ɛksploˈzjoːn]
fight	**Schlägerei** [ʃlɛːgəˈʀaɪ]

Call the police!	**Rufen Sie die Polizei!** [ʀuːfən ziː di ˌpoliˈtsaɪ!]
Please hurry up!	**Schneller bitte!** [ʃnɛlɐ ˈbɪtə!]
I'm looking for the police station.	**Ich suche nach einer Polizeistation.** [ɪç ˈzuːχə naːχ ˈaɪnə poliˈtsaɪʃtaˌtsjoːn]
I need to make a call.	**Ich muss einen Anruf tätigen.** [ɪç mʊs ˈaɪnən ˈanˌʀuːf ˈtɛːtɪgən]
May I use your phone?	**Kann ich Ihr Telefon benutzen?** [kan ɪç iːɐ teleˈfoːn bəˈnʊtsən?]

I've been ...	**Ich wurde ...** [ɪç ˈvʊʁdə ...]
mugged	**ausgeraubt** [aʊsgəˌʀaʊpt]
robbed	**überfallen** [ˌyːbɐˈfalən]
raped	**vergewaltigt** [fɛɐgəˈvaltɪçt]
attacked (beaten up)	**angegriffen** [angəˌgʀɪfən]

Are you all right?	**Ist bei Ihnen alles in Ordnung?** [ist baɪ ˈiːnən ˈaləs ɪn ˈɔʁdnʊŋ?]
Did you see who it was?	**Haben Sie gesehen wer es war?** [haːbən ziː geˈzeːən veːɐ ɛs vaːɐ?]
Would you be able to recognize the person?	**Sind Sie in der Lage die Person wiederzuerkennen?** [zɪnt ziː ɪn deːɐ laːgə di pɛʁˈzoːn ˈviːdetsuʔɛɐˌkɛnən?]
Are you sure?	**Sind sie sicher?** [zɪnt ziː ˈzɪçɐ?]

Please calm down.	**Beruhigen Sie sich bitte!** [bəˈʀuːɪgən ziː zɪç ˈbɪtə!]
Take it easy!	**Ruhig!** [ʀuːɪç!]
Don't worry!	**Machen Sie sich keine Sorgen.** [maχən ziː zɪç ˈkaɪnə ˈzɔʁgən]
Everything will be fine.	**Alles wird gut.** [aləs vɪʁt guːt]
Everything's all right.	**Alles ist in Ordnung.** [aləs ist ɪn ˈɔʁdnʊŋ]

Come here, please.

Kommen Sie bitte her.
[kɔmən zi: 'bɪtə he:ɐ]

I have some questions for you.

Ich habe einige Fragen für Sie.
[ɪç 'ha:bə 'aɪnɪgə 'fʀa:gən fy:ɐ zi:]

Wait a moment, please.

Warten Sie einen Moment bitte.
[vaʁtən 'aɪnən mo'mɛnt 'bɪtə]

Do you have any I.D.?

Haben Sie einen Ausweis?
[ha:bən zi: 'aɪnən 'aʊsˌvaɪs?]

Thanks. You can leave now.

Danke. Sie können nun gehen.
[daŋkə. zi: 'kœnən nu:n 'ge:ən]

Hands behind your head!

Hände hinter dem Kopf!
[hɛndə 'hɪntɐ dem kɔpf!]

You're under arrest!

Sie sind verhaftet!
[zi: zɪnt fɛɐ'haftət!]

Health problems

Please help me.	**Helfen Sie mir bitte.** [hɛlfən ziː miːɐ 'bɪtə]
I don't feel well.	**Mir ist schlecht.** [miːɐ ɪs ʃlɛçt]
My husband doesn't feel well.	**Meinem Ehemann ist schlecht.** [maɪnəm 'eːəman ist ʃlɛçt]
My son ...	**Mein Sohn ...** [maɪn zoːn ...]
My father ...	**Mein Vater ...** [maɪn 'faːtɐ ...]

My wife doesn't feel well.	**Meine Frau fühlt sich nicht gut.** [maɪnə 'fʀaʊ fyːlt zɪç nɪçt guːt]
My daughter ...	**Meine Tochter ...** [maɪnə 'tɔxtɐ ...]
My mother ...	**Meine Mutter ...** [maɪnə 'mʊtɐ ...]

I've got a ...	**Ich habe ... schmerzen.** [ɪç 'haːbə ... 'ʃmɛʀtsən]
headache	**Kopf-** [kɔpf]
sore throat	**Hals-** [hals]
stomach ache	**Bauch-** [baʊx]
toothache	**Zahn-** [tsaːn]

I feel dizzy.	**Mir ist schwindelig.** [miːɐ ɪs 'ʃvɪndəlɪç]
He has a fever.	**Er hat Fieber.** [eːɐ hat 'fiːbɐ]
She has a fever.	**Sie hat Fieber.** [ziː hat 'fiːbɐ]
I can't breathe.	**Ich kann nicht atmen.** [ɪç kan nɪçt 'aːtmən]

I'm short of breath.	**Ich kriege keine Luft.** [ɪç 'kʀiːgə 'kaɪnə lʊft]
I am asthmatic.	**Ich bin Asthmatiker.** [ɪç bɪn ast'maːtikɐ]
I am diabetic.	**Ich bin Diabetiker /Diabetikerin/** [ɪç bɪn dia'beːtikɐ /dia'beːtikəʀɪn/]

I can't sleep.	**Ich habe Schlaflosigkeit.** [ɪç 'haːbə 'ʃlaːfloːzɪçkaɪt]
food poisoning	**Lebensmittelvergiftung** [leːbəns‚mɪtəl·fɛɐ‚gɪftʊŋ]

It hurts here.	**Es tut hier weh.** [ɛs tʊt hiːɐ veː]
Help me!	**Hilfe!** [hɪlfə!]
I am here!	**Ich bin hier!** [ɪç bɪn hiːɐ!]
We are here!	**Wir sind hier!** [viːɐ zɪnt hiːɐ!]
Get me out of here!	**Bringen Sie mich hier raus!** [bʀɪŋən ziː mɪç hiːɐ 'ʀaʊs!]
I need a doctor.	**Ich brauche einen Arzt.** [ɪç 'bʀaʊxə 'aɪnən aʁtst]
I can't move.	**Ich kann mich nicht bewegen.** [ɪç kan mɪç nɪçt bə'veːgən]
I can't move my legs.	**Ich kann meine Beine nicht bewegen.** [ɪç kan 'maɪnə 'baɪnə nɪçt bə'veːgən]

I have a wound.	**Ich habe eine Wunde.** [ɪç 'haːbə 'aɪnə 'vʊndə]
Is it serious?	**Ist es ernst?** [ist ɛs ɛʁnst?]
My documents are in my pocket.	**Meine Dokumente sind in meiner Hosentasche.** [maɪnə doku'mɛntə zɪnt ɪn 'maɪnə 'hoːzən‚taʃə]
Calm down!	**Beruhigen Sie sich!** [bə'ʀuːɪgən ziː zɪç!]
May I use your phone?	**Kann ich Ihr Telefon benutzen?** [kan ɪç iːɐ tele'foːn bə'nʊtsən?]

Call an ambulance!	**Rufen Sie einen Krankenwagen!** [ʀuːfən ziː 'aɪnən 'kʀaŋkən‚vaːgən!]
It's urgent!	**Es ist dringend!** [ɛs ist 'dʀɪŋənt!]
It's an emergency!	**Es ist ein Notfall!** [ɛs ist aɪn 'noːt‚fal!]
Please hurry up!	**Schneller bitte!** [ʃnɛlɐ 'bɪtə!]
Would you please call a doctor?	**Können Sie bitte einen Arzt rufen?** [kœnən ziː 'bɪtə 'aɪnən aʁtst 'ʀuːfən?]
Where is the hospital?	**Wo ist das Krankenhaus?** [voː ist das 'kʀaŋkən‚haʊs?]

How are you feeling?	**Wie fühlen Sie sich?** [viː 'fyːlən ziː zɪç?]
Are you all right?	**Ist bei Ihnen alles in Ordnung?** [ist baɪ 'iːnən 'aləs ɪn 'ɔʁdnʊŋ?]

What's happened?

Was ist passiert?
[vas ɪst pa'siːɐt?]

I feel better now.

Mir geht es schon besser.
[miːɐ geːt ɛs ʃoːn 'bɛsɐ]

It's OK.

Es ist in Ordnung.
[ɛs ist ɪn 'ɔʁdnʊŋ]

It's all right.

Alles ist in Ordnung.
[aləs ist ɪn 'ɔʁdnʊŋ]

At the pharmacy

pharmacy (drugstore)	**Apotheke** [apoˈteːkə]
24-hour pharmacy	**24 Stunden Apotheke** [fiːɐ·ʊn·ˈtsvantsɪç ˈʃtʊndən apoˈteːkə]
Where is the closest pharmacy?	**Wo ist die nächste Apotheke?** [voː ist di ˈnɛːçstə apoˈteːkə?]
Is it open now?	**Ist sie jetzt offen?** [ist ziː jɛtst ˈɔfən?]
At what time does it open?	**Um wie viel Uhr öffnet sie?** [ʊm vifiːl uːɐ ˈœfnət ziː?]
At what time does it close?	**Um wie viel Uhr schließt sie?** [ʊm vifiːl uːɐ ʃliːst ziː?]
Is it far?	**Ist es weit?** [ist ɛs vaɪt?]
Can I get there on foot?	**Kann ich dort zu Fuß hingehen?** [kan ɪç dɔʁt tsu fuːs ˈhɪnˌgeːən?]
Can you show me on the map?	**Können Sie es mir auf der Karte zeigen?** [kœnən ziː ɛs miːɐ aʊf deːɐ ˈkaʁtə ˈtsaɪgən?]
Please give me something for ...	**Bitte geben sie mir etwas gegen ...** [bɪtə geːbn ziː miːɐ ˈɛtvas ˈgeːgən ...]
a headache	**Kopfschmerzen** [kɔpfˌʃmɛʁtsən]
a cough	**Husten** [huːstən]
a cold	**eine Erkältung** [aɪnə ɛɐˈkɛltʊŋ]
the flu	**die Grippe** [di ˈgʁɪpə]
a fever	**Fieber** [fiːbɐ]
a stomach ache	**Magenschmerzen** [maːgənˌʃmɛʁtsən]
nausea	**Übelkeit** [yːbəlkaɪt]
diarrhea	**Durchfall** [dʊʁçˌfal]
constipation	**Verstopfung** [fɛɐˈʃtɔpfʊŋ]

pain in the back	**Rückenschmerzen**
	[ʀʏkən‿ʃmɛʁtsən]
chest pain	**Brustschmerzen**
	[bʀʊstʃmɛʁtsən]
side stitch	**Seitenstechen**
	[zaɪtənʃtɛçən]
abdominal pain	**Bauchschmerzen**
	[baʊχʃmɛʁtsən]

pill	**Pille**
	[pɪlə]
ointment, cream	**Salbe, Creme**
	[zalbə, kʀɛːm]
syrup	**Sirup**
	[ziːʀʊp]
spray	**Spray**
	[ʃpʀeː]
drops	**Tropfen**
	[tʀɔpfən]

You need to go to the hospital.	**Sie müssen ins Krankenhaus gehen.**
	[ziː ˈmʏsən ɪns ˈkʀaŋkənˌhaʊs ˈgeːən]
health insurance	**Krankenversicherung**
	[kʀaŋkən·fɛɐ̯ˌzɪçəʀʊŋ]
prescription	**Rezept**
	[ʀe̯ˈtsɛpt]
insect repellant	**Insektenschutzmittel**
	[ɪnˈzɛktən·ˈʃʊtsˌmɪtəl]
Band Aid	**Pflaster**
	[pflastɐ]

The bare minimum

Excuse me, ...	**Entschuldigen Sie bitte, ...** [ɛntˈʃʊldɪgən ziː ˈbɪtə, ...]
Hello.	**Hallo.** [haˈloː]
Thank you.	**Danke.** [daŋkə]
Good bye.	**Auf Wiedersehen.** [aʊf ˈviːdɐˌzeːən]
Yes.	**Ja.** [jaː]
No.	**Nein.** [naɪn]
I don't know.	**Ich weiß nicht.** [ɪç vaɪs nɪçt]
Where? | Where to? | When?	**Wo? | Wohin? | Wann?** [voː? | voˈhɪn? | van?]
I need ...	**Ich brauche ...** [ɪç ˈbʀaʊxə ...]
I want ...	**Ich möchte ...** [ɪç ˈmœçtə ...]
Do you have ...?	**Haben Sie ...?** [haːbən ziː ...?]
Is there a ... here?	**Gibt es hier ...?** [giːpt ɛs hiːɐ ...?]
May I ...?	**Kann ich ...?** [kan ɪç ...?]
..., please (polite request)	**Bitte** [bɪtə]
I'm looking for ...	**Ich suche ...** [ɪç ˈzuːxə ...]
the restroom	**Toilette** [toaˈlɛtə]
an ATM	**Geldautomat** [gɛltʔaʊtoˌmaːt]
a pharmacy (drugstore)	**Apotheke** [apoˈteːkə]
a hospital	**Krankenhaus** [kʀaŋkənˌhaʊs]
the police station	**Polizeistation** [poliˈtsaɪˌʃtaˌtsjoːn]
the subway	**U-Bahn** [uːbaːn]

a taxi	**Taxi** [taksi]
the train station	**Bahnhof** [baːnˌhoːf]

My name is ...	**Ich heiße ...** [ɪç 'haɪsə ...]
What's your name?	**Wie heißen Sie?** [viː 'haɪsən ziː?]
Could you please help me?	**Helfen Sie mir bitte.** [hɛlfən ziː miːɐ 'bɪtə]
I've got a problem.	**Ich habe ein Problem.** [ɪç 'haːbə aɪn pʀo'bleːm]
I don't feel well.	**Mir ist schlecht.** [miːɐ ɪs ʃlɛçt]
Call an ambulance!	**Rufen Sie einen Krankenwagen!** [ʀuːfən ziː 'aɪnən 'kʀaŋkənˌvaːgən!]
May I make a call?	**Darf ich telefonieren?** [daʁf ɪç telefo'niːʀən?]

I'm sorry.	**Entschuldigung.** [ɛnt'ʃʊldɪgʊŋ]
You're welcome.	**Keine Ursache.** [kaɪnə 'uːɐˌzaχə]

I, me	**ich** [ɪç]
you (inform.)	**du** [duː]
he	**er** [eːɐ]
she	**sie** [ziː]
they (masc.)	**sie** [ziː]
they (fem.)	**sie** [ziː]
we	**wir** [viːɐ]
you (pl)	**ihr** [iːɐ]
you (sg, form.)	**Sie** [ziː]

ENTRANCE	**EINGANG** [aɪnˌgaŋ]
EXIT	**AUSGANG** [aʊsˌgaŋ]
OUT OF ORDER	**AUßER BETRIEB** [ˌaʊsɐ bə'tʀiːp]
CLOSED	**GESCHLOSSEN** [gə'ʃlɔsən]

OPEN   **OFFEN**
                        [ɔfən]

FOR WOMEN   **FÜR DAMEN**
                        [fyːɐ 'damən]

FOR MEN   **FÜR HERREN**
                        [fyːɐ 'hɛʀən]

CONCISE
DICTIONARY

This section contains more
than 1,500 useful words
arranged alphabetically.
The dictionary includes a lot
of gastronomic terms and
will be helpful when ordering
food at a restaurant or buying
groceries

T&P Books Publishing

DICTIONARY CONTENTS

T&P Books Publishing

1. Time. Calendar

time	**Zeit** (f)	[tsaɪt]
hour	**Stunde** (f)	[ˈʃtʊndə]
half an hour	**eine halbe Stunde**	[ˈaɪnə ˈhalbə ˈʃtʊndə]
minute	**Minute** (f)	[miˈnuːtə]
second	**Sekunde** (f)	[zeˈkʊndə]
today (adv)	**heute**	[ˈhɔɪtə]
tomorrow (adv)	**morgen**	[ˈmɔʁɡən]
yesterday (adv)	**gestern**	[ˈɡɛstɐn]
Monday	**Montag** (m)	[ˈmoːntaːk]
Tuesday	**Dienstag** (m)	[ˈdiːnstaːk]
Wednesday	**Mittwoch** (m)	[ˈmɪtvɔχ]
Thursday	**Donnerstag** (m)	[ˈdɔnɐstaːk]
Friday	**Freitag** (m)	[ˈfʁaɪtaːk]
Saturday	**Samstag** (m)	[ˈzamstaːk]
Sunday	**Sonntag** (m)	[ˈzɔntaːk]
day	**Tag** (m)	[taːk]
working day	**Arbeitstag** (m)	[ˈaʁbaɪtsˌtaːk]
public holiday	**Feiertag** (m)	[ˈfaɪɐˌtaːk]
weekend	**Wochenende** (n)	[ˈvɔχənˌʔɛndə]
week	**Woche** (f)	[ˈvɔχə]
last week (adv)	**letzte Woche**	[ˈlɛtstə ˈvɔχə]
next week (adv)	**nächste Woche**	[ˈnɛːçstə ˈvɔχə]
sunrise	**Sonnenaufgang** (m)	[ˈzɔnənˌʔaʊfɡaŋ]
sunset	**Sonnenuntergang** (m)	[ˈzɔnənˌʔʊntɐɡaŋ]
in the morning	**morgens**	[ˈmɔʁɡəns]
in the afternoon	**nachmittags**	[ˈnaːχmɪˌtaːks]
in the evening	**abends**	[ˈaːbənts]
tonight (this evening)	**heute Abend**	[ˈhɔɪtə ˈaːbənt]
at night	**nachts**	[naχts]
midnight	**Mitternacht** (f)	[ˈmɪtɐˌnaχt]
January	**Januar** (m)	[ˈjanuaːɐ]
February	**Februar** (m)	[ˈfeːbʁuaːɐ]
March	**März** (m)	[mɛʁts]
April	**April** (m)	[aˈpʁɪl]
May	**Mai** (m)	[maɪ]
June	**Juni** (m)	[ˈjuːni]

July	Juli (m)	['ju:li]
August	August (m)	[aʊ'gʊst]
September	September (m)	[zɛp'tɛmbɐ]
October	Oktober (m)	[ɔk'to:bɐ]
November	November (m)	[no'vɛmbɐ]
December	Dezember (m)	[de'tsɛmbɐ]

in spring	im Frühling	[ɪm 'fʀy:lɪŋ]
in summer	im Sommer	[ɪm 'zɔmɐ]
in fall	im Herbst	[ɪm hɛʁpst]
in winter	im Winter	[ɪm 'vɪntɐ]

month	Monat (m)	['mo:nat]
season (summer, etc.)	Saison (f)	[zɛ'zɔŋ]
year	Jahr (n)	[ja:ɐ]
century	Jahrhundert (n)	[ja:ɐ'hʊndɐt]

2. Numbers. Numerals

digit, figure	Ziffer (f)	['tsɪfɐ]
number	Zahl (f)	[tsa:l]
minus sign	Minus (n)	['mi:nʊs]
plus sign	Plus (n)	[plʊs]
sum, total	Summe (f)	['zʊmə]

first (adj)	der erste	[de:ɐ 'ɛʁstə]
second (adj)	der zweite	[de:ɐ 'tsvaɪtə]
third (adj)	der dritte	[de:ɐ 'dʀɪtə]

0 zero	null	[nʊl]
1 one	eins	[aɪns]
2 two	zwei	[tsvaɪ]
3 three	drei	[dʀaɪ]
4 four	vier	[fi:ɐ]

5 five	fünf	[fʏnf]
6 six	sechs	[zɛks]
7 seven	sieben	['zi:bən]
8 eight	acht	[aχt]
9 nine	neun	[nɔɪn]
10 ten	zehn	[tse:n]

11 eleven	elf	[ɛlf]
12 twelve	zwölf	[tsvœlf]
13 thirteen	dreizehn	['dʀaɪtse:n]
14 fourteen	vierzehn	['fɪʁtse:n]
15 fifteen	fünfzehn	['fʏnftse:n]

| 16 sixteen | sechzehn | ['zɛçtse:n] |
| 17 seventeen | siebzehn | ['zi:ptse:n] |

| 18 eighteen | achtzehn | [ˈaχtseːn] |
| 19 nineteen | neunzehn | [ˈnɔɪntseːn] |

20 twenty	zwanzig	[ˈtsvantsɪç]
30 thirty	dreißig	[ˈdʀaɪsɪç]
40 forty	vierzig	[ˈfiʁtsɪç]
50 fifty	fünfzig	[ˈfʏnftsɪç]

60 sixty	sechzig	[ˈzɛçtsɪç]
70 seventy	siebzig	[ˈziːptsɪç]
80 eighty	achtzig	[ˈaχtsɪç]
90 ninety	neunzig	[ˈnɔɪntsɪç]

100 one hundred	einhundert	[ˈaɪnˌhʊndet]
200 two hundred	zweihundert	[ˈtsvaɪˌhʊndet]
300 three hundred	dreihundert	[ˈdʀaɪˌhʊndet]
400 four hundred	vierhundert	[ˈfiːɐˌhʊndet]
500 five hundred	fünfhundert	[ˈfʏnfˌhʊndet]

600 six hundred	sechshundert	[zɛksˌhʊndet]
700 seven hundred	siebenhundert	[ˈziːbənˌhʊndet]
800 eight hundred	achthundert	[ˈaχtˌhʊndet]
900 nine hundred	neunhundert	[ˈnɔɪnˌhʊndet]
1000 one thousand	eintausend	[ˈaɪnˌtaʊzənt]

| 10000 ten thousand | zehntausend | [ˈtsenˌtaʊzənt] |
| one hundred thousand | hunderttausend | [ˈhʊndetˌtaʊzənt] |

| million | Million (f) | [mɪˈljoːn] |
| billion | Milliarde (f) | [mɪˈlɪaʁdə] |

3. Humans. Family

man (adult male)	Mann (m)	[man]
young man	Junge (m)	[ˈjʊŋə]
teenager	Teenager (m)	[ˈtiːneːdʒe]
woman	Frau (f)	[fʀaʊ]
girl (young woman)	Mädchen (n)	[ˈmɛːtçən]

age	Alter (n)	[ˈaltə]
adult (adj)	Erwachsene (f)	[ɛɐˈvaksənə]
middle-aged (adj)	in mittleren Jahren	[ɪn ˈmɪtləʀən ˈjaːʀən]
elderly (adj)	älterer	[ˈɛltəʀɐ]
old (adj)	alt	[alt]

old man	Greis (m)	[gʀaɪs]
old woman	alte Frau (f)	[ˈaltə ˈfʀaʊ]
retirement	Ruhestand (m)	[ˈʀuːəˌʃtant]
to retire (from job)	in Rente gehen	[ɪn ˈʀɛntə ˈgeːən]
retiree	Rentner (m)	[ˈʀɛntnɐ]

mother	Mutter (f)	['mʊtə]
father	Vater (m)	['faːtɐ]
son	Sohn (m)	[zoːn]
daughter	Tochter (f)	['tɔχtɐ]
brother	Bruder (m)	['bʀuːdɐ]
sister	Schwester (f)	['ʃvɛstɐ]

parents	Eltern (pl)	['ɛltɐn]
child	Kind (n)	[kɪnt]
children	Kinder (pl)	['kɪndɐ]
stepmother	Stiefmutter (f)	['ʃtiːfˌmʊtə]
stepfather	Stiefvater (m)	['ʃtiːfˌfaːtə]

grandmother	Großmutter (f)	['gʀoːsˌmʊtə]
grandfather	Großvater (m)	['gʀoːsˌfaːtə]
grandson	Enkel (m)	['ɛŋkəl]
granddaughter	Enkelin (f)	['ɛŋkəlɪn]
grandchildren	Enkelkinder (pl)	['ɛŋkəlˌkɪndə]

uncle	Onkel (m)	['ɔŋkəl]
aunt	Tante (f)	['tantə]
nephew	Neffe (m)	['nɛfə]
niece	Nichte (f)	['nɪçtə]

wife	Frau (f)	[fʀaʊ]
husband	Mann (m)	[man]
married (masc.)	verheiratet	[fɛɐ'haɪʀaːtət]
married (fem.)	verheiratet	[fɛɐ'haɪʀaːtət]
widow	Witwe (f)	['vɪtvə]
widower	Witwer (m)	['vɪtvə]

| name (first name) | Vorname (m) | ['foːɐˌnaːmə] |
| surname (last name) | Name (m) | ['naːmə] |

relative	Verwandte (m)	[fɛɐ'vantə]
friend (masc.)	Freund (m)	[fʀɔɪnt]
friendship	Freundschaft (f)	['fʀɔɪntʃaft]

partner	Partner (m)	['paʁtnə]
superior (n)	Vorgesetzte (m)	['foːɐgəˌzɛtstə]
colleague	Kollege (m), Kollegin (f)	[kɔ'leːgə], [kɔ'leːgɪn]
neighbors	Nachbarn (pl)	['naχbaːɐn]

4. Human body

organism (body)	Organismus (m)	[ˌɔʁga'nɪsmʊs]
body	Körper (m)	['kœʁpə]
heart	Herz (n)	[hɛʁts]
blood	Blut (n)	[bluːt]
brain	Gehirn (n)	[gə'hɪʁn]

nerve	**Nerv** (m)	[nɛʁf]
bone	**Knochen** (m)	['knɔχən]
skeleton	**Skelett** (n)	[ske'lɛt]
spine (backbone)	**Wirbelsäule** (f)	['vɪʁbəl‚zɔɪlə]
rib	**Rippe** (f)	['ʁɪpə]
skull	**Schädel** (m)	['ʃɛːdəl]
muscle	**Muskel** (m)	['mʊskəl]
lungs	**Lungen** (pl)	['lʊŋən]
skin	**Haut** (f)	[haʊt]
head	**Kopf** (m)	[kɔpf]
face	**Gesicht** (n)	[gə'zɪçt]
nose	**Nase** (f)	['naːzə]
forehead	**Stirn** (f)	[ʃtɪʁn]
cheek	**Wange** (f)	['vaŋə]
mouth	**Mund** (m)	[mʊnt]
tongue	**Zunge** (f)	['tsʊŋə]
tooth	**Zahn** (m)	[tsaːn]
lips	**Lippen** (pl)	['lɪpən]
chin	**Kinn** (n)	[kɪn]
ear	**Ohr** (n)	[oːɐ]
neck	**Hals** (m)	[hals]
throat	**Kehle** (f)	['keːlə]
eye	**Auge** (n)	['aʊgə]
pupil	**Pupille** (f)	[pu'pɪlə]
eyebrow	**Augenbraue** (f)	['aʊgən‚bʁaʊə]
eyelash	**Wimper** (f)	['vɪmpɐ]
hair	**Haare** (pl)	['haːʁə]
hairstyle	**Frisur** (f)	[‚fʁi'zuːɐ]
mustache	**Schnurrbart** (m)	['ʃnʊʁ‚baːɐt]
beard	**Bart** (m)	[baːɐt]
to have (a beard, etc.)	**haben** (vt)	['haːbən]
bald (adj)	**kahl**	[kaːl]
hand	**Hand** (f)	[hant]
arm	**Arm** (m)	[aʁm]
finger	**Finger** (m)	['fɪŋɐ]
nail	**Nagel** (m)	['naːgəl]
palm	**Handfläche** (f)	['hant·‚flɛçə]
shoulder	**Schulter** (f)	['ʃʊltɐ]
leg	**Bein** (n)	[baɪn]
foot	**Fuß** (m)	[fuːs]
knee	**Knie** (n)	[kniː]
heel	**Ferse** (f)	['fɛʁzə]
back	**Rücken** (m)	['ʁʏkən]
waist	**Taille** (f)	['taljə]

beauty mark	**Leberfleck** (m)	['leːbɐˌflɛk]
birthmark	**Muttermal** (n)	['mʊtɐˌmaːl]
(café au lait spot)		

5. Medicine. Diseases. Drugs

health	**Gesundheit** (f)	[gə'zʊnthaɪt]
well (not sick)	**gesund**	[gə'zʊnt]
sickness	**Krankheit** (f)	['kʀaŋkhaɪt]
to be sick	**krank sein**	[kʀaŋk zaɪn]
ill, sick (adj)	**krank**	[kʀaŋk]

cold (illness)	**Erkältung** (f)	[ɛɐ'kɛltʊŋ]
to catch a cold	**sich erkälten**	[zɪç ɛɐ'kɛltən]
tonsillitis	**Angina** (f)	[aŋ'giːna]
pneumonia	**Lungenentzündung** (f)	['lʊŋənʔɛntˌtsʏndʊŋ]
flu, influenza	**Grippe** (f)	['gʀɪpə]

runny nose (coryza)	**Schnupfen** (m)	['ʃnʊpfən]
cough	**Husten** (m)	['huːstən]
to cough (vi)	**husten** (vi)	['huːstən]
to sneeze (vi)	**niesen** (vi)	['niːzən]

stroke	**Schlaganfall** (m)	['ʃlaːkʔanˌfal]
heart attack	**Infarkt** (m)	[ɪn'faʁkt]
allergy	**Allergie** (f)	[ˌalɛʁ'giː]
asthma	**Asthma** (n)	['astma]
diabetes	**Diabetes** (m)	[dia'beːtɛs]

tumor	**Tumor** (m)	['tuːmoːɐ]
cancer	**Krebs** (m)	[kʀeːps]
alcoholism	**Alkoholismus** (m)	[ˌalkoho'lɪsmʊs]
AIDS	**AIDS**	['eɪts]
fever	**Fieber** (n)	['fiːbɐ]
seasickness	**Seekrankheit** (f)	['zeːˌkʀaŋkhaɪt]

bruise (hématome)	**blauer Fleck** (m)	['blaʊɐ flɛk]
bump (lump)	**Beule** (f)	['bɔɪlə]
to limp (vi)	**hinken** (vi)	['hɪŋkən]
dislocation	**Verrenkung** (f)	[fɛɐ'ʀɛnkʊŋ]
to dislocate (vt)	**ausrenken** (vt)	['aʊsˌʀɛŋkən]

fracture	**Fraktur** (f)	[fʀak'tuːɐ]
burn (injury)	**Verbrennung** (f)	[fɛɐ'bʀɛnʊŋ]
injury	**Verletzung** (f)	[fɛɐ'lɛtsʊŋ]
pain, ache	**Schmerz** (m)	[ʃmɛʁts]
toothache	**Zahnschmerz** (m)	['tsaːnˌʃmɛʁts]

| to sweat (perspire) | **schwitzen** (vi) | ['ʃvɪtsən] |
| deaf (adj) | **taub** | [taʊp] |

mute (adj)	**stumm**	[ʃtʊm]
immunity	**Immunität** (f)	[ɪmuni'tɛ:t]
virus	**Virus** (m, n)	['vi:ʀʊs]
microbe	**Mikrobe** (f)	[mi'kʀo:bə]
bacterium	**Bakterie** (f)	[bak'te:ʀɪə]
infection	**Infektion** (f)	[ɪnfɛk'tsjo:n]
hospital	**Krankenhaus** (n)	['kʀaŋkən,haʊs]
cure	**Heilung** (f)	['haɪlʊŋ]
to vaccinate (vt)	**impfen** (vt)	['ɪmpfən]
to be in a coma	**im Koma liegen**	[ɪm 'ko:ma 'li:gən]
intensive care	**Reanimation** (f)	[ʀeʔanima'tsjo:n]
symptom	**Symptom** (n)	[zʏmp'to:m]
pulse	**Puls** (m)	[pʊls]

6. Feelings. Emotions. Conversation

I, me	**ich**	[ɪç]
you	**du**	[du:]
he	**er**	[e:ɐ]
she	**sie**	[zi:]
it	**es**	[ɛs]
we	**wir**	[vi:ɐ]
you (to a group)	**ihr**	[i:ɐ]
you (polite, sing.)	**Sie**	[zi:]
you (polite, pl)	**Sie**	[zi:]
they	**sie**	[zi:]
Hello! (fam.)	**Hallo!**	[ha'lo:]
Hello! (form.)	**Hallo!**	[ha'lo:]
Good morning!	**Guten Morgen!**	['gu:tən 'mɔʀgən]
Good afternoon!	**Guten Tag!**	['gu:tən 'ta:k]
Good evening!	**Guten Abend!**	['gu:tən 'a:bənt]
to say hello	**grüßen** (vi, vt)	['gʀy:sən]
to greet (vt)	**begrüßen** (vt)	[bə'gʀy:sən]
How are you?	**Wie geht's?**	[,vi: 'ge:ts]
Bye-Bye! Goodbye!	**Auf Wiedersehen!**	[aʊf 'vi:dɐ,ze:ən]
Thank you!	**Danke!**	['daŋkə]
feelings	**Gefühle** (pl)	[gə'fy:lə]
to be hungry	**hungrig sein**	['hʊŋʀɪç zaɪn]
to be thirsty	**Durst haben**	['dʊʀst 'ha:bən]
tired (adj)	**müde**	['my:də]
to be worried	**sorgen** (vi)	['zɔʀgən]
to be nervous	**nervös sein**	[nɛʀ'vø:s zaɪn]
hope	**Hoffnung** (f)	['hɔfnʊŋ]
to hope (vi, vt)	**hoffen** (vi)	['hɔfən]

character	Charakter (m)	[ka'ʀaktɐ]
modest (adj)	bescheiden	[bə'ʃaɪdən]
lazy (adj)	faul	[faʊl]
generous (adj)	freigebig	['fʀaɪˌge:bɪç]
talented (adj)	talentiert	[talɛn'ti:ɐt]

honest (adj)	ehrlich	['e:ɐlɪç]
serious (adj)	ernst	[ɛʀnst]
shy, timid (adj)	schüchtern	['ʃʏçtɐn]
sincere (adj)	aufrichtig	['aʊfˌʀɪçtɪç]
coward	Feigling (m)	['faɪklɪŋ]

to sleep (vi)	schlafen (vi)	['ʃla:fən]
dream	Traum (m)	[tʀaʊm]
bed	Bett (n)	[bɛt]
pillow	Kissen (n)	['kɪsən]

insomnia	Schlaflosigkeit (f)	['ʃla:flo:zɪçkaɪt]
to go to bed	schlafen gehen	['ʃla:fən 'ge:ən]
nightmare	Alptraum (m)	['alpˌtʀaʊm]
alarm clock	Wecker (m)	['vɛkɐ]

smile	Lächeln (n)	['lɛçəln]
to smile (vi)	lächeln (vi)	['lɛçəln]
to laugh (vi)	lachen (vi)	['laxən]

quarrel	Zank (m)	[tsaŋk]
insult	Kränkung (f)	['kʀɛŋkʊŋ]
resentment	Beleidigung (f)	[bə'laɪdɪgʊŋ]
angry (mad)	verärgert	[fɛɐ'ɛʀgɐt]

7. Clothing. Personal accessories

clothes	Kleidung (f)	['klaɪdʊŋ]
coat (overcoat)	Mantel (m)	['mantəl]
fur coat	Pelzmantel (m)	['pɛltsˌmantəl]
jacket (e.g., leather ~)	Jacke (f)	['jakə]
raincoat (trenchcoat, etc.)	Regenmantel (m)	['ʀe:gənˌmantəl]

shirt (button shirt)	Hemd (n)	[hɛmt]
pants	Hose (f)	['ho:zə]
suit jacket	Jackett (n)	[ʒa'kɛt]
suit	Anzug (m)	['anˌtsu:k]

dress (frock)	Kleid (n)	[klaɪt]
skirt	Rock (m)	[ʀɔk]
T-shirt	T-Shirt (n)	['ti:ˌʃø:ɐt]
bathrobe	Bademantel (m)	['ba:dəˌmantəl]
pajamas	Schlafanzug (m)	['ʃla:f?anˌtsu:k]
workwear	Arbeitskleidung (f)	['aʀbaɪtsˌklaɪdʊŋ]

underwear	Unterwäsche (f)	['ʊntɐˌvɛʃə]
socks	Socken (pl)	['zɔkən]
bra	Büstenhalter (m)	['bystənˌhaltɐ]
pantyhose	Strumpfhose (f)	['ʃtʀʊmpfˌho:zə]
stockings (thigh highs)	Strümpfe (pl)	['ʃtʀʏmpfə]
bathing suit	Badeanzug (m)	['ba:dəˌʔantsu:k]
hat	Mütze (f)	['mʏtsə]
footwear	Schuhe (pl)	['ʃu:ə]
boots (e.g., cowboy ~)	Stiefel (pl)	['ʃti:fəl]
heel	Absatz (m)	['apˌzats]
shoestring	Schnürsenkel (m)	['ʃnyːɐˌsɛŋkəl]
shoe polish	Schuhcreme (f)	['ʃu:ˌkʀɛ:m]
cotton (n)	Baumwolle (f)	['baʊmˌvɔlə]
wool (n)	Wolle (f)	['vɔlə]
fur (n)	Pelz (m)	[pɛlts]
gloves	Handschuhe (pl)	['hantˌʃu:ə]
mittens	Fausthandschuhe (pl)	['faʊst·hantˌʃu:ə]
scarf (muffler)	Schal (m)	[ʃa:l]
glasses (eyeglasses)	Brille (f)	['bʀɪlə]
umbrella	Regenschirm (m)	['ʀe:gənˌʃɪʀm]
tie (necktie)	Krawatte (f)	[kʀa'vatə]
handkerchief	Taschentuch (n)	['taʃənˌtu:χ]
comb	Kamm (m)	[kam]
hairbrush	Haarbürste (f)	['ha:ɐˌbʏʀstə]
buckle	Schnalle (f)	['ʃnalə]
belt	Gürtel (m)	['gʏʀtəl]
purse	Handtasche (f)	['hantˌtaʃə]
collar	Kragen (m)	['kʀa:gən]
pocket	Tasche (f)	['taʃə]
sleeve	Ärmel (m)	['ɛʀməl]
fly (on trousers)	Hosenschlitz (m)	['ho:zənˌʃlɪts]
zipper (fastener)	Reißverschluss (m)	['ʀaɪs·fɛɐˌʃlʊs]
button	Knopf (m)	[knɔpf]
to get dirty (vi)	sich beschmutzen	[zɪç bə'ʃmʊtsən]
stain (mark, spot)	Fleck (m)	[flɛk]

8. City. Urban institutions

store	Laden (m)	['la:dən]
shopping mall	Einkaufszentrum (n)	['aɪnkaʊfsˌtsɛntʀʊm]
supermarket	Supermarkt (m)	['zu:pɐˌmaʀkt]
shoe store	Schuhgeschäft (n)	['ʃu:gəˌʃɛft]
bookstore	Buchhandlung (f)	['bu:χˌhandlʊŋ]

drugstore, pharmacy	**Apotheke** (f)	[apoˈteːkə]
bakery	**Bäckerei** (f)	[ˌbɛkəˈʁaɪ]
pastry shop	**Konditorei** (f)	[ˌkɔndɪtoˈʁaɪ]
grocery store	**Lebensmittelladen** (m)	[ˈleːbənsˌmɪtəlˈlaːdən]
butcher shop	**Metzgerei** (f)	[mɛtsgəˈʁaɪ]
produce store	**Gemüseladen** (m)	[gəˈmyːzəˌlaːdən]
market	**Markt** (m)	[maʁkt]

hair salon	**Friseursalon** (m)	[fʁiˈzøːɐ·zaˌlɔn]
post office	**Post** (f)	[pɔst]
dry cleaners	**chemische Reinigung** (f)	[çeˈmiʃə ˈʁaɪnɪgʊn]
circus	**Zirkus** (m)	[ˈtsɪʁkʊs]
zoo	**Zoo** (m)	[ˈtsoː]

theater	**Theater** (n)	[teˈaːtɐ]
movie theater	**Kino** (n)	[ˈkiːno]
museum	**Museum** (n)	[muˈzeːʊm]
library	**Bibliothek** (f)	[biblioˈteːk]

mosque	**Moschee** (f)	[mɔˈʃeː]
synagogue	**Synagoge** (f)	[zynaˈgoːgə]
cathedral	**Kathedrale** (f)	[kateˈdʁaːlə]
temple	**Tempel** (m)	[ˈtɛmpəl]
church	**Kirche** (f)	[ˈkɪʁçə]

college	**Institut** (n)	[ɪnstiˈtuːt]
university	**Universität** (f)	[univɛʁziˈtɛːt]
school	**Schule** (f)	[ˈʃuːlə]

hotel	**Hotel** (n)	[hoˈtɛl]
bank	**Bank** (f)	[baŋk]
embassy	**Botschaft** (f)	[ˈboːtʃaft]
travel agency	**Reisebüro** (n)	[ˈʁaɪzə·byˌʁoː]

subway	**U-Bahn** (f)	[ˈuːbaːn]
hospital	**Krankenhaus** (n)	[ˈkʁaŋkənˌhaʊs]
gas station	**Tankstelle** (f)	[ˈtaŋkʃtɛlə]
parking lot	**Parkplatz** (m)	[ˈpaʁkˌplats]

ENTRANCE	**EINGANG**	[ˈaɪnˌgaŋ]
EXIT	**AUSGANG**	[ˈaʊsˌgaŋ]
PUSH	**DRÜCKEN**	[ˈdʁʏkən]
PULL	**ZIEHEN**	[ˈtsiːən]
OPEN	**GEÖFFNET**	[gəˈʔœfnət]
CLOSED	**GESCHLOSSEN**	[gəˈʃlɔsən]

monument	**Denkmal** (n)	[ˈdɛŋkˌmaːl]
fortress	**Festung** (f)	[ˈfɛstʊn]
palace	**Palast** (m)	[paˈlast]

medieval (adj)	**mittelalterlich**	[ˈmɪtəlˌʔaltəlɪç]
ancient (adj)	**alt**	[alt]

| national (adj) | **national** | [natsjɔ'naːl] |
| famous (monument, etc.) | **berühmt** | [bə'ʀyːmt] |

9. Money. Finances

money	**Geld** (n)	[gɛlt]
coin	**Münze** (f)	['mʏntsə]
dollar	**Dollar** (m)	['dɔlaʁ]
euro	**Euro** (m)	['ɔɪʀo]

ATM	**Geldautomat** (m)	['gɛltʔauto͵maːt]
currency exchange	**Wechselstube** (f)	['vɛksəlˌʃtuːbə]
exchange rate	**Kurs** (m)	[kuʁs]
cash	**Bargeld** (n)	['baːɐ̯ˌgɛlt]

How much?	**Wie viel?**	['viː fiːl]
to pay (vi, vt)	**zahlen** (vt)	['tsaːlən]
payment	**Lohn** (m)	[loːn]
change (give the ~)	**Wechselgeld** (n)	['vɛksəlˌgɛlt]

price	**Preis** (m)	[pʀaɪs]
discount	**Rabatt** (m)	[ʀa'bat]
cheap (adj)	**billig**	['bɪlɪç]
expensive (adj)	**teuer**	['tɔɪɐ]

bank	**Bank** (f)	[baŋk]
account	**Konto** (n)	['kɔnto]
credit card	**Kreditkarte** (f)	[kʀe'diːtˌkaʁtə]
check	**Scheck** (m)	[ʃɛk]
to write a check	**einen Scheck schreiben**	['aɪnən ʃɛk 'ʃʀaɪbn]
checkbook	**Scheckbuch** (n)	['ʃɛkˌbuːχ]

debt	**Schuld** (f)	[ʃult]
debtor	**Schuldner** (m)	['ʃuldnɐ]
to lend (money)	**leihen** (vt)	['laɪən]
to borrow (vi, vt)	**ausleihen** (vt)	['ausˌlaɪən]

to rent (~ a tuxedo)	**ausleihen** (vt)	['ausˌlaɪən]
on credit (adv)	**auf Kredit**	[auf kʀe'diːt]
wallet	**Geldtasche** (f)	['gɛltˌtaʃə]
safe	**Safe** (m)	[sɛɪf]
inheritance	**Erbschaft** (f)	['ɛʁpʃaft]
fortune (wealth)	**Vermögen** (n)	[fɛɐ'møːgən]

tax	**Steuer** (f)	['ʃtɔɪɐ]
fine	**Geldstrafe** (f)	['gɛltˌʃtʀaːfə]
to fine (vt)	**bestrafen** (vt)	[bə'ʃtʀaːfən]

| wholesale (adj) | **Großhandels-** | ['gʀoːsˌhandəls] |
| retail (adj) | **Einzelhandels-** | ['aɪntsəlˌhandəls] |

to insure (vt)	versichern (vt)	[fɛɐ̯'zɪçən]
insurance	Versicherung (f)	[fɛɐ̯'zɪçərʊŋ]
capital	Kapital (n)	[kapi'ta:l]
turnover	Umsatz (m)	['ʊmˌzats]
stock (share)	Aktie (f)	['aktsiə]
profit	Gewinn (m)	[gə'vɪn]
profitable (adj)	gewinnbringend	[gə'vɪnˌbrɪŋənt]
crisis	Krise (f)	['kri:zə]
bankruptcy	Bankrott (m)	[baŋ'krɔt]
to go bankrupt	Bankrott machen	[baŋ'krɔt 'maχən]
accountant	Buchhalter (m)	['bu:χˌhaltə]
salary	Lohn (m)	[lo:n]
bonus (money)	Prämie (f)	['prɛ:miə]

10. Transportation

bus	Bus (m)	[bʊs]
streetcar	Straßenbahn (f)	['ʃtra:sənˌba:n]
trolley bus	Obus (m)	['o:bʊs]
to go by ...	mit ... fahren	[mɪt ... 'fa:ʀən]
to get on (~ the bus)	einsteigen (vi)	['aɪnˌʃtaɪgən]
to get off ...	aussteigen (vi)	['aʊsˌʃtaɪgən]
stop (e.g., bus ~)	Haltestelle (f)	['haltəˌʃtɛlə]
terminus	Endhaltestelle (f)	['ɛntˌhaltəʃtɛlə]
schedule	Fahrplan (m)	['fa:ɐ̯ˌpla:n]
ticket	Fahrkarte (f)	['fa:ɐ̯ˌkaʁtə]
to be late (for ...)	sich verspäten	[zɪç fɛɐ̯'ʃpɛ:tən]
taxi, cab	Taxi (n)	['taksi]
by taxi	mit dem Taxi	[mɪt dem 'taksi]
taxi stand	Taxistand (m)	['taksiˌʃtant]
traffic	Straßenverkehr (m)	['ʃtra:sən·fɛɐ̯ˌke:ɐ̯]
rush hour	Hauptverkehrszeit (f)	['haʊpt·fɛɐ̯'ke:ɐsˌtsaɪt]
to park (vi)	parken (vi)	['paʁkən]
subway	U-Bahn (f)	['u:ba:n]
station	Station (f)	[ʃta'tsjo:n]
train	Zug (m)	[tsu:k]
train station	Bahnhof (m)	['ba:nˌho:f]
rails	Schienen (pl)	['ʃi:nən]
compartment	Abteil (n)	[ap'taɪl]
berth	Liegeplatz (m),	['li:gəˌplats],
	Schlafkoje (f)	['ʃla:fˌko:jə]
airplane	Flugzeug (n)	['flu:kˌtsɔɪk]

air ticket	Flugticket (n)	['flu:kˌtɪkət]
airline	Fluggesellschaft (f)	['flu:kgəˌzɛlʃaft]
airport	Flughafen (m)	['flu:kˌha:fən]

flight (act of flying)	Flug (m)	[flu:k]
luggage	Gepäck (n)	[gə'pɛk]
luggage cart	Kofferkuli (m)	['kɔfeˌku:li]

ship	Schiff (n)	[ʃɪf]
cruise ship	Kreuzfahrtschiff (n)	['kʀɔɪtsfa:etˌʃɪf]
yacht	Jacht (f)	[jaxt]
boat (flat-bottomed ~)	Boot (n)	['bo:t]

captain	Kapitän (m)	[kapi'tɛn]
cabin	Kajüte (f)	[ka'jy:tə]
port (harbor)	Hafen (m)	['ha:fən]

bicycle	Fahrrad (n)	['fa:eˌʀa:t]
scooter	Motorroller (m)	['mo:to:eˌʀɔlə]
motorcycle, bike	Motorrad (n)	['mo:to:eˌʀa:t]
pedal	Pedal (n)	[pe'da:l]
pump	Pumpe (f)	['pʊmpə]
wheel	Rad (n)	[ʀa:t]

automobile, car	Auto (n)	['aʊto]
ambulance	Krankenwagen (m)	['kʀaŋkənˌva:gən]
truck	Lastkraftwagen (m)	['lastkʀaftˌva:gən]
used (adj)	gebraucht	[gə'bʀaʊxt]
car crash	Unfall (m)	['ʊnfal]
repair	Reparatur (f)	[ʀepaʀa'tu:ɐ]

11. Food. Part 1

meat	Fleisch (n)	[flaɪʃ]
chicken	Hühnerfleisch (n)	['hy:neˌflaɪʃ]
duck	Ente (f)	['ɛntə]

pork	Schweinefleisch (n)	['ʃvaɪnəˌflaɪʃ]
veal	Kalbfleisch (n)	['kalpˌflaɪʃ]
lamb	Hammelfleisch (n)	['haməlˌflaɪʃ]
beef	Rindfleisch (n)	['ʀɪntˌflaɪʃ]

sausage (bologna, pepperoni, etc.)	Wurst (f)	[vʊʀst]
egg	Ei (n)	[aɪ]
fish	Fisch (m)	[fɪʃ]
cheese	Käse (m)	['kɛ:zə]
sugar	Zucker (m)	['tsʊkɐ]
salt	Salz (n)	[zalts]
rice	Reis (m)	[ʀaɪs]

pasta (macaroni)	**Teigwaren** (pl)	['taɪkˌvaːʀən]
butter	**Butter** (f)	['bʊtɐ]
vegetable oil	**Pflanzenöl** (n)	['pflantsənˌʔøːl]
bread	**Brot** (n)	[bʀoːt]
chocolate (n)	**Schokolade** (f)	[ʃoko'laːdə]

wine	**Wein** (m)	[vaɪn]
coffee	**Kaffee** (m)	['kafe]
milk	**Milch** (f)	[mɪlç]
juice	**Saft** (m)	[zaft]
beer	**Bier** (n)	[biːɐ]
tea	**Tee** (m)	[teː]

tomato	**Tomate** (f)	[to'maːtə]
cucumber	**Gurke** (f)	['gʊʀkə]
carrot	**Karotte** (f)	[ka'ʀɔtə]
potato	**Kartoffel** (f)	[kaʀ'tɔfəl]
onion	**Zwiebel** (f)	['tsviːbəl]
garlic	**Knoblauch** (m)	['knoːpˌlaʊχ]

cabbage	**Kohl** (m)	[koːl]
beetroot	**Zuckerrübe** (f)	['tsʊkɐˌʀyːbə]
eggplant	**Aubergine** (f)	[ˌobɛʀ'ʒiːnə]
dill	**Dill** (m)	[dɪl]
lettuce	**Kopf Salat** (m)	[kɔpf za'laːt]
corn (maize)	**Mais** (m)	['maɪs]

fruit	**Frucht** (f)	[fʀʊχt]
apple	**Apfel** (m)	['apfəl]
pear	**Birne** (f)	['bɪʀnə]
lemon	**Zitrone** (f)	[tsi'tʀoːnə]
orange	**Apfelsine** (f)	[apfəl'ziːnə]
strawberry (garden ~)	**Erdbeere** (f)	['eːɐtˌbeːʀə]

plum	**Pflaume** (f)	['pflaʊmə]
raspberry	**Himbeere** (f)	['hɪmˌbeːʀə]
pineapple	**Ananas** (f)	['ananas]
banana	**Banane** (f)	[ba'naːnə]
watermelon	**Wassermelone** (f)	['vasɛmeˌloːnə]
grape	**Weintrauben** (pl)	['vaɪnˌtʀaʊbən]
melon	**Melone** (f)	[me'loːnə]

12. Food. Part 2

cuisine	**Küche** (f)	['kʏçə]
recipe	**Rezept** (n)	[ʀe'tsɛpt]
food	**Essen** (n)	['ɛsən]

to have breakfast	**frühstücken** (vi)	['fʀyːʃtʏkən]
to have lunch	**zu Mittag essen**	[tsʊ 'mɪtaːk 'ɛsən]

to have dinner	zu Abend essen	[tsu 'a:bənt 'ɛsən]
taste, flavor	Geschmack (m)	[gə'ʃmak]
tasty (adj)	lecker	['lɛkɐ]
cold (adj)	kalt	[kalt]
hot (adj)	heiß	[haɪs]
sweet (sugary)	süß	[zy:s]
salty (adj)	salzig	['zaltsɪç]

sandwich (bread)	belegtes Brot (n)	[bə'le:ktəs bʀo:t]
side dish	Beilage (f)	['baɪ,la:gə]
filling (for cake, pie)	Füllung (f)	['fʏlʊŋ]
sauce	Soße (f)	['zo:sə]
piece (of cake, pie)	Stück (n)	[ʃtʏk]

diet	Diät (f)	[di'ɛ:t]
vitamin	Vitamin (n)	[vita'mi:n]
calorie	Kalorie (f)	[kalo'ʀi:]
vegetarian (n)	Vegetarier (m)	[vege'ta:ʀiɐ]

restaurant	Restaurant (n)	[ʀɛsto'ʀaŋ]
coffee house	Kaffeehaus (n)	[ka'fe:,haʊs]
appetite	Appetit (m)	[ape'ti:t]
Enjoy your meal!	Guten Appetit!	[,gutən ,?ape'ti:t]
waiter	Kellner (m)	['kɛlnɐ]
waitress	Kellnerin (f)	['kɛlnəʀɪn]
bartender	Barmixer (m)	['ba:ɐ,mɪksɐ]
menu	Speisekarte (f)	['ʃpaɪzə,kaʀtə]

spoon	Löffel (m)	['lœfəl]
knife	Messer (n)	['mɛsɐ]
fork	Gabel (f)	[ga:bəl]
cup (e.g., coffee ~)	Tasse (f)	['tasə]

plate (dinner ~)	Teller (m)	['tɛlɐ]
saucer	Untertasse (f)	['ʊntɐ,tasə]
napkin (on table)	Serviette (f)	[zɛʀ'viɛtə]
toothpick	Zahnstocher (m)	['tsa:nʃtɔχɐ]

to order (meal)	bestellen (vt)	[bə'ʃtɛlən]
course, dish	Gericht (n)	[gə'ʀɪçt]
portion	Portion (f)	[pɔʀ'tsjo:n]
appetizer	Vorspeise (f)	['fo:ɐʃpaɪzə]
salad	Salat (m)	[za'la:t]
soup	Suppe (f)	['zʊpə]

dessert	Nachtisch (m)	['na:χ,tɪʃ]
jam (whole fruit jam)	Konfitüre (f)	[,kɔnfi'ty:ʀə]
ice-cream	Eis (n)	[aɪs]

check	Rechnung (f)	['ʀɛçnʊŋ]
to pay the check	Rechnung bezahlen	['ʀɛçnʊŋ bə'tsa:lən]
tip	Trinkgeld (n)	['tʀɪŋk,gɛlt]

13. House. Apartment. Part 1

house	**Haus** (n)	[haʊs]
country house	**Landhaus** (n)	['lantˌhaʊs]
villa (seaside ~)	**Villa** (f)	['vɪla]

floor, story	**Stock** (m)	[ʃtɔk]
entrance	**Eingang** (m)	['aɪnˌgaŋ]
wall	**Wand** (f)	[vant]
roof	**Dach** (n)	[daχ]
chimney	**Rohr** (n)	[ʀoːɐ]

attic (storage place)	**Dachboden** (m)	['daχˌboːdən]
window	**Fenster** (n)	['fɛnstɐ]
window ledge	**Fensterbrett** (n)	['fɛnstɐˌbʀɛt]
balcony	**Balkon** (m)	[bal'koːn]

stairs (stairway)	**Treppe** (f)	['tʀɛpə]
mailbox	**Briefkasten** (m)	['bʀiːfˌkastən]
garbage can	**Müllkasten** (m)	['mʏlˌkastən]
elevator	**Aufzug** (m), **Fahrstuhl** (m)	['aʊfˌtsuːk], ['faːɐˌʃtuːl]

electricity	**Elektrizität** (f)	[elɛktʀitsi'tɛːt]
light bulb	**Glühbirne** (f)	['glyːˌbɪʁnə]
switch	**Schalter** (m)	['ʃaltɐ]
wall socket	**Steckdose** (f)	['ʃtɛkˌdoːzə]
fuse	**Sicherung** (f)	['zɪçəʀʊŋ]

door	**Tür** (f)	[tyːɐ]
handle, doorknob	**Griff** (m)	[gʀɪf]
key	**Schlüssel** (m)	['ʃlʏsəl]
doormat	**Fußmatte** (f)	['fuːsˌmatə]

door lock	**Schloss** (n)	[ʃlɔs]
doorbell	**Türklingel** (f)	['tyːɐˌklɪŋəl]
knock (at the door)	**Klopfen** (n)	['klɔpfən]
to knock (vi)	**anklopfen** (vi)	['anˌklɔpfən]
peephole	**Türspion** (m)	['tyːɐˌʃpiˌoːn]

yard	**Hof** (m)	[hoːf]
garden	**Garten** (m)	['gaʁtən]
swimming pool	**Schwimmbad** (n)	['ʃvɪmbaːt]
gym (home gym)	**Kraftraum** (m)	['kʀaftˌʀaʊm]
tennis court	**Tennisplatz** (m)	['tɛnɪsˌplats]
garage	**Garage** (f)	[ga'ʀaːʒə]

private property	**Privateigentum** (n)	[pʀi'vaːtˌʔaɪgəntuːm]
warning sign	**Warnschild** (n)	['vaʁnˌʃɪlt]
security	**Bewachung** (f)	[bə'vaχʊŋ]
security guard	**Wächter** (m)	['vɛçtɐ]
renovations	**Renovierung** (f)	[ʀeno'viːʀʊŋ]

to renovate (vt)	renovieren (vt)	[ʀeno'viːʀən]
to put in order	in Ordnung bringen	[ɪn 'ɔʀdnʊŋ 'bʀɪŋən]
to paint (~ a wall)	streichen (vt)	['ʃtʀaɪçən]
wallpaper	Tapete (f)	[ta'peːtə]
to varnish (vt)	lackieren (vt)	[la'kiːʀən]
pipe	Rohr (n)	[ʀoːɐ]
tools	Werkzeuge (pl)	['vɛʀkˌtsɔɪɡə]
basement	Keller (m)	['kɛlɐ]
sewerage (system)	Kanalisation (f)	[kanaliza'tsjoːn]

14. House. Apartment. Part 2

apartment	Wohnung (f)	['voːnʊŋ]
room	Zimmer (n)	['tsɪmɐ]
bedroom	Schlafzimmer (n)	['ʃlaːfˌtsɪmɐ]
dining room	Esszimmer (n)	['ɛsˌtsɪmɐ]
living room	Wohnzimmer (n)	['voːnˌtsɪmɐ]
study (home office)	Arbeitszimmer (n)	['aʀbaɪtsˌtsɪmɐ]
entry room	Vorzimmer (n)	['foːɐˌtsɪmɐ]
bathroom (room with a bath or shower)	Badezimmer (n)	['baːdəˌtsɪmɐ]
half bath	Toilette (f)	[toa'lɛtə]
floor	Fußboden (m)	['fuːsˌboːdən]
ceiling	Decke (f)	['dɛkə]
to dust (vt)	Staub abwischen	[ʃtaʊp 'apˌvɪʃən]
vacuum cleaner	Staubsauger (m)	['ʃtaʊpˌzaʊɡɐ]
to vacuum (vt)	Staub saugen	[ʃtaʊp 'zaʊɡən]
mop	Schrubber (m)	['ʃʀʊbɐ]
dust cloth	Lappen (m)	['lapən]
short broom	Besen (m)	['beːzən]
dustpan	Kehrichtschaufel (f)	['keːʀɪçtˌʃaʊfəl]
furniture	Möbel (n)	['møːbəl]
table	Tisch (m)	[tɪʃ]
chair	Stuhl (m)	[ʃtuːl]
armchair	Sessel (m)	['zɛsəl]
bookcase	Bücherschrank (m)	['byːçɐˌʃʀaŋk]
shelf	Regal (n)	[ʀe'ɡaːl]
wardrobe	Schrank (m)	[ʃʀaŋk]
mirror	Spiegel (m)	['ʃpiːɡəl]
carpet	Teppich (m)	['tɛpɪç]
fireplace	Kamin (m)	[ka'miːn]
drapes	Vorhänge (pl)	['foːɐhɛŋə]

| table lamp | **Tischlampe** (f) | ['tɪʃˌlampə] |
| chandelier | **Kronleuchter** (m) | ['kʀoːnˌlɔɪçtə] |

kitchen	**Küche** (f)	['kʏçə]
gas stove (range)	**Gasherd** (m)	['gaːsˌheːɐt]
electric stove	**Elektroherd** (m)	[e'lɛktʀoˌheːɐt]
microwave oven	**Mikrowellenherd** (m)	['mikʀovɛlənˌheːɐt]

refrigerator	**Kühlschrank** (m)	['kyːlˌʃʀaŋk]
freezer	**Tiefkühltruhe** (f)	['tiːfkyːlˌtʀuːə]
dishwasher	**Geschirrspülmaschine** (f)	[gə'ʃɪʀˈʃpyːlˈmaˌʃiːnə]
faucet	**Wasserhahn** (m)	['vasəˌhaːn]

meat grinder	**Fleischwolf** (m)	['flaɪˌʃvolf]
juicer	**Saftpresse** (f)	['zaftˌpʀɛsə]
toaster	**Toaster** (m)	['toːstə]
mixer	**Mixer** (m)	['mɪksə]

coffee machine	**Kaffeemaschine** (f)	['kafeˈmaˌʃiːnə]
kettle	**Wasserkessel** (m)	['vasəˌkɛsəl]
teapot	**Teekanne** (f)	['teːˌkanə]

TV set	**Fernseher** (m)	['fɛʀnˌzeːɐ]
VCR (video recorder)	**Videorekorder** (m)	['videoˈʀeˌkɔʀdə]
iron (e.g., steam ~)	**Bügeleisen** (n)	['byːgəlˌʔaɪzən]
telephone	**Telefon** (n)	[tele'foːn]

15. Professions. Social status

director	**Direktor** (m)	[di'ʀɛktoːɐ]
superior	**Vorgesetzte** (m)	['foːɐgəˌzɛtstə]
president	**Präsident** (m)	[pʀɛzi'dɛnt]
assistant	**Helfer** (m)	['hɛlfə]
secretary	**Sekretär** (m)	[zekʀe'tɛːɐ]

owner, proprietor	**Besitzer** (m)	[bə'zɪtsə]
partner	**Partner** (m)	['paʀtnə]
stockholder	**Aktionär** (m)	[aktsjo'nɛːɐ]

businessman	**Geschäftsmann** (m)	[gə'ʃɛftsˌman]
millionaire	**Millionär** (m)	[mɪljo'nɛːɐ]
billionaire	**Milliardär** (m)	[ˌmɪliaʀ'dɛːɐ]

actor	**Schauspieler** (m)	['ʃaʊʃpiːlə]
architect	**Architekt** (m)	[aʀçi'tɛkt]
banker	**Bankier** (m)	[baŋ'kɪeː]
broker	**Makler** (m)	['maːklə]

| veterinarian | **Tierarzt** (m) | ['tiːɐˌʔaʀtst] |
| doctor | **Arzt** (m) | [aʀtst] |

chambermaid	**Zimmermädchen** (n)	['tsɪmɐˌmɛːtçən]
designer	**Designer** (m)	[di'zaɪnɐ]
correspondent	**Korrespondent** (m)	[kɔʀɛspɔn'dɛnt]
delivery man	**Ausfahrer** (m)	['aʊsˌfaːʀɐ]
electrician	**Elektriker** (m)	[ˌe'lɛktʀikɐ]
musician	**Musiker** (m)	['muːzikɐ]
babysitter	**Kinderfrau** (f)	['kɪndɐˌfʀaʊ]
hairdresser	**Friseur** (m)	[fʀi'zøːɐ]
herder, shepherd	**Hirt** (m)	[hɪʀt]
singer (masc.)	**Sänger** (m)	['zɛŋɐ]
translator	**Übersetzer** (m)	[ˌyːbɐ'zɛtsɐ]
writer	**Schriftsteller** (m)	['ʃʀɪftˌʃtɛlɐ]
carpenter	**Zimmermann** (m)	['tsɪmɐˌman]
cook	**Koch** (m)	[kɔχ]
fireman	**Feuerwehrmann** (m)	['fɔɪveːeˌman]
police officer	**Polizist** (m)	[poli'tsɪst]
mailman	**Briefträger** (m)	['bʀiːfˌtʀɛːgɐ]
programmer	**Programmierer** (m)	[pʀogʀa'miːʀɐ]
salesman (store staff)	**Verkäufer** (m)	[fɛɐ'kɔɪfɐ]
worker	**Arbeiter** (m)	['aʀbaɪtɐ]
gardener	**Gärtner** (m)	['gɛʀtnɐ]
plumber	**Klempner** (m)	['klɛmpnɐ]
dentist	**Zahnarzt** (m)	['tsaːnˌʔaʀtst]
flight attendant (fem.)	**Flugbegleiterin** (f)	['fluːkˌbəˌglaɪtəʀɪn]
dancer (masc.)	**Tänzer** (m)	['tɛntsɐ]
bodyguard	**Leibwächter** (m)	['laɪpˌvɛçtɐ]
scientist	**Wissenschaftler** (m)	['vɪsənˌʃaftlɐ]
schoolteacher	**Lehrer** (m)	['leːʀɐ]
farmer	**Farmer** (m)	['faʀmɐ]
surgeon	**Chirurg** (m)	[çi'ʀʊʀk]
miner	**Bergarbeiter** (m)	['bɛʀkʔaʀˌbaɪtɐ]
chef (kitchen chef)	**Chefkoch** (m)	['ʃɛfˌkɔχ]
driver	**Fahrer** (m)	['faːʀɐ]

16. Sport

kind of sports	**Sportart** (f)	['ʃpɔʀtʔaːɐt]
soccer	**Fußball** (m)	['fuːsbal]
hockey	**Eishockey** (n)	['aɪsˌhɔki]
basketball	**Basketball** (m)	['baːskətbal]
baseball	**Baseball** (m, n)	['bɛɪsbɔːl]
volleyball	**Volleyball** (m)	['vɔliˌbal]
boxing	**Boxen** (n)	['bɔksən]

wrestling	**Ringen** (n)	['ʀɪŋən]
tennis	**Tennis** (n)	['tɛnɪs]
swimming	**Schwimmen** (n)	['ʃvɪmən]
chess	**Schach** (n)	[ʃaχ]
running	**Lauf** (m)	[laʊf]
athletics	**Leichtathletik** (f)	['laɪçt?atˌle:tik]
figure skating	**Eiskunstlauf** (m)	['aɪskʊnstˌlaʊf]
cycling	**Radfahren** (n)	['ʀa:tˌfa:ʀən]
billiards	**Billard** (n)	['bɪljaʀt]
bodybuilding	**Bodybuilding** (n)	['bɔdiˌbɪldɪŋ]
golf	**Golf** (n)	[gɔlf]
scuba diving	**Tauchen** (n)	['taʊχən]
sailing	**Segelsport** (m)	['ze:gəlˌʃpɔʀt]
archery	**Bogenschießen** (n)	['bo:gənˌʃi:sən]
period, half	**Halbzeit** (f)	['halpˌtsaɪt]
half-time	**Halbzeit** (f), **Pause** (f)	['halpˌtsaɪt], ['paʊzə]
tie	**Unentschieden** (n)	['ʊn?ɛntˌʃi:dən]
to tie (vi)	**unentschieden spielen**	['ʊn?ɛntˌʃi:dən 'ʃpi:lən]
treadmill	**Laufbahn** (f)	['laʊfˌba:n]
player	**Spieler** (m)	['ʃpi:lɐ]
substitute	**Ersatzspieler** (m)	[ɛɐ'zatsˌʃpi:lɐ]
substitutes bench	**Ersatzbank** (f)	[ɛɐ'zatsˌbaŋk]
match	**Spiel** (n)	[ʃpi:l]
goal	**Tor** (n)	[to:ɐ]
goalkeeper	**Torwart** (m)	['to:ɐˌvaʀt]
goal (score)	**Tor** (n)	[to:ɐ]
Olympic Games	**Olympische Spiele** (pl)	[o'lʏmpɪʃə 'ʃpi:lə]
to set a record	**einen Rekord aufstellen**	['aɪnən ʀe'kɔʀt 'aʊfˌʃtɛlən]
final	**Finale** (n)	[fi'na:lə]
champion	**Meister** (m)	['maɪstɐ]
championship	**Meisterschaft** (f)	['maɪstɐˌʃaft]
winner	**Sieger** (m)	['zi:gɐ]
victory	**Sieg** (m)	[zi:k]
to win (vi)	**gewinnen** (vt)	[gə'vɪnən]
to lose (not win)	**verlieren** (vt)	[fɛɐ'li:ʀən]
medal	**Medaille** (f)	[me'daljə]
first place	**der erste Platz**	[de:ɐ 'ɛʀstə plats]
second place	**der zweite Platz**	[de:ɐ 'tsvaɪtə plats]
third place	**der dritte Platz**	[de:ɐ 'dʀɪtə plats]
stadium	**Stadion** (n)	['ʃta:djɔn]
fan, supporter	**Fan** (m)	[fɛn]
trainer, coach	**Trainer** (m)	['tʀɛ:nɐ]
training	**Training** (n)	['tʀɛ:nɪŋ]

17. Foreign languages. Orthography

language	**Sprache** (f)	['ʃpʀaːχə]
to study (vt)	**studieren** (vt)	[ʃtuˈdiːʀən]
pronunciation	**Aussprache** (f)	['aʊsˌʃpʀaːχə]
accent	**Akzent** (m)	[akˈtsɛnt]
noun	**Substantiv** (n)	['zʊpstantiːf]
adjective	**Adjektiv** (n)	['atjɛktiːf]
verb	**Verb** (n)	[vɛʀp]
adverb	**Adverb** (n)	[atˈvɛʀp]
pronoun	**Pronomen** (n)	[pʀoˈnoːmən]
interjection	**Interjektion** (f)	[ˌɪntɐjɛkˈtsjoːn]
preposition	**Präposition** (f)	[pʀɛpoziˈtsjoːn]
root	**Wurzel** (f)	['vʊʀtsəl]
ending	**Endung** (f)	['ɛndʊŋ]
prefix	**Vorsilbe** (f)	['foːɐˌzɪlbə]
syllable	**Silbe** (f)	['zɪlbə]
suffix	**Suffix** (n), **Nachsilbe** (f)	['zʊfɪks], ['naːχˌzɪlbə]
stress mark	**Betonung** (f)	[bəˈtoːnʊŋ]
period, dot	**Punkt** (m)	[pʊŋkt]
comma	**Komma** (n)	['kɔma]
colon	**Doppelpunkt** (m)	['dɔpəlˌpʊŋkt]
ellipsis	**Auslassungspunkte** (pl)	['aʊslasʊŋsˌpʊŋktə]
question	**Frage** (f)	['fʀaːgə]
question mark	**Fragezeichen** (n)	['fʀaːgəˌtsaɪçən]
exclamation point	**Ausrufezeichen** (n)	['aʊsʀuːfəˌtsaɪçən]
in quotation marks	**in Anführungszeichen**	[ɪn 'anfyːʀʊŋsˌtsaɪçən]
in parenthesis	**in Klammern**	[ɪn 'klamɐn]
letter	**Buchstabe** (m)	['buːχˌʃtaːbə]
capital letter	**Großbuchstabe** (m)	['gʀoːsbuːχˌʃtaːbə]
sentence	**Satz** (m)	[zats]
group of words	**Wortverbindung** (f)	['vɔʀtfɛɐˌbɪndʊŋ]
expression	**Redensart** (f)	['ʀeːdənsˌʔaːɐt]
subject	**Subjekt** (n)	['zʊpjɛkt]
predicate	**Prädikat** (n)	[pʀɛdiˈkaːt]
line	**Zeile** (f)	['tsaɪlə]
paragraph	**Absatz** (m)	['apˌzats]
synonym	**Synonym** (n)	[zynoˈnyːm]
antonym	**Antonym** (n)	[antoˈnyːm]
exception	**Ausnahme** (f)	['aʊsˌnaːmə]
to underline (vt)	**unterstreichen** (vt)	[ˌʊntɐˈʃtʀaɪçən]
rules	**Regeln** (pl)	['ʀeːgəln]

grammar	Grammatik (f)	[gʀa'matɪk]
vocabulary	Vokabular (n)	[vokabu'la:ɐ]
phonetics	Phonetik (f)	[fo:'ne:tɪk]
alphabet	Alphabet (n)	[alfa'be:t]

textbook	Lehrbuch (n)	['le:ɐˌbu:x]
dictionary	Wörterbuch (n)	['vœɐtɐˌbu:x]
phrasebook	Sprachführer (m)	['ʃpʀa:xˌfy:ʀɐ]

word	Wort (n)	[vɔʀt]
meaning	Bedeutung (f)	[bɐ'dɔɪtʊŋ]
memory	Gedächtnis (n)	[gɐ'dɛçtnɪs]

18. The Earth. Geography

the Earth	Erde (f)	['e:ɐdə]
the globe (the Earth)	Erdkugel (f)	['e:ɐt·ku:gəl]
planet	Planet (m)	[pla'ne:t]

geography	Geographie (f)	[ˌgeogʀa'fi:]
nature	Natur (f)	[na'tu:ɐ]
map	Landkarte (f)	['lantˌkaʀtə]
atlas	Atlas (m)	['atlas]

in the north	im Norden	[ɪm 'nɔʀdən]
in the south	im Süden	[ɪm 'zy:dən]
in the west	im Westen	[ɪm 'vɛstən]
in the east	im Osten	[ɪm 'ɔstən]

sea	Meer (n), See (f)	[me:ɐ], [ze:]
ocean	Ozean (m)	['o:tsea:n]
gulf (bay)	Bucht (f)	[bʊxt]
straits	Meerenge (f)	['me:ɐˌʔɛŋə]

continent (mainland)	Kontinent (m)	['kɔntinɛnt]
island	Insel (f)	['ɪnzəl]
peninsula	Halbinsel (f)	['halpˌʔɪnzəl]
archipelago	Archipel (m)	[ˌaʀçi'pe:l]

harbor	Hafen (m)	['ha:fən]
coral reef	Korallenriff (n)	[ko'ʀalənˌʀɪf]
shore	Ufer (n)	['u:fɐ]
coast	Küste (f)	['kʏstə]

| flow (flood tide) | Flut (f) | [flu:t] |
| ebb (ebb tide) | Ebbe (f) | ['ɛbə] |

latitude	Breite (f)	['bʀaɪtə]
longitude	Länge (f)	['lɛŋə]
parallel	Parallele (f)	[paʀa'le:lə]

equator	Äquator (m)	[ɛ'kvaːtoːɐ]
sky	Himmel (m)	['hɪməl]
horizon	Horizont (m)	[hoʀi'tsɔnt]
atmosphere	Atmosphäre (f)	[ʔatmo'sfɛːʀə]
mountain	Berg (m)	[bɛʀk]
summit, top	Gipfel (m)	['gɪpfəl]
cliff	Fels (m)	[fɛls]
hill	Hügel (m)	['hyːgəl]
volcano	Vulkan (m)	[vʊl'kaːn]
glacier	Gletscher (m)	['glɛtʃɐ]
waterfall	Wasserfall (m)	['vasɐˌfal]
plain	Ebene (f)	['eːbənə]
river	Fluss (m)	[flʊs]
spring (natural source)	Quelle (f)	['kvɛlə]
bank (of river)	Ufer (n)	['uːfɐ]
downstream (adv)	stromabwärts	['ʃtʀoːmˌapvɛʀts]
upstream (adv)	stromaufwärts	['ʃtʀoːmˌaʊfvɛʀts]
lake	See (m)	[zeː]
dam	Damm (m)	[dam]
canal	Kanal (m)	[ka'naːl]
swamp (marshland)	Sumpf (m), Moor (n)	[zʊmpf], [moːɐ]
ice	Eis (n)	[aɪs]

19. Countries of the world. Part 1

Europe	Europa (n)	[ɔɪ'ʀoːpa]
European Union	Europäische Union (f)	[ˌɔɪʀo'pɛːɪʃə ʔu'njoːn]
European (n)	Europäer (m)	[ˌɔɪʀo'pɛːɐ]
European (adj)	europäisch	[ˌɔɪʀo'pɛːɪʃ]
Austria	Österreich (n)	['øːstəʀaɪç]
Great Britain	Großbritannien (n)	[gʀoːs·bʀi'tanɪən]
England	England (n)	['ɛŋlant]
Belgium	Belgien (n)	['bɛlgɪən]
Germany	Deutschland (n)	['dɔɪtʃlant]
Netherlands	Niederlande (f)	['niːdɐˌlandə]
Holland	Holland (n)	['hɔlant]
Greece	Griechenland (n)	['gʀiːçənˌlant]
Denmark	Dänemark (n)	['dɛːnəˌmaʀk]
Ireland	Irland (n)	['ɪʀlant]
Iceland	Island (n)	['iːslant]
Spain	Spanien (n)	['ʃpaːnɪən]
Italy	Italien (n)	[i'taːlɪən]
Cyprus	Zypern (n)	['tsyːpɐn]

Malta	Malta (n)	['malta]
Norway	Norwegen (n)	['nɔʁˌveːɡən]
Portugal	Portugal (n)	['pɔʁtugal]
Finland	Finnland (n)	['fɪnlant]
France	Frankreich (n)	['fʁaŋkʁaɪç]
Sweden	Schweden (n)	['ʃveːdən]

Switzerland	Schweiz (f)	[ʃvaɪts]
Scotland	Schottland (n)	['ʃɔtlant]
Vatican	Vatikan (m)	[vati'kaːn]
Liechtenstein	Liechtenstein (n)	['lɪçtənˌʃtaɪn]
Luxembourg	Luxemburg (n)	['lʊksəmˌbʊʁk]

Monaco	Monaco (n)	[mo'nako]
Albania	Albanien (n)	[al'baːniən]
Bulgaria	Bulgarien (n)	[bʊl'gaːʁiən]
Hungary	Ungarn (n)	['ʊŋgaʁn]
Latvia	Lettland (n)	['lɛtlant]

Lithuania	Litauen (n)	['lɪtaʊən]
Poland	Polen (n)	['poːlən]
Romania	Rumänien (n)	[ʁu'mɛːniən]
Serbia	Serbien (n)	['zɛʁbiən]
Slovakia	Slowakei (f)	[slova'kaɪ]

Croatia	Kroatien (n)	[kʁo'aːtsiən]
Czech Republic	Tschechien (n)	['tʃɛçiən]
Estonia	Estland (n)	['ɛstlant]
Bosnia and Herzegovina	Bosnien und Herzegowina (n)	['bɔsniən ʊnt ˌhɛʁtsə'goːvinaː]
Macedonia (Republic of ~)	Makedonien (n)	[makeˈdoːniən]

Slovenia	Slowenien (n)	[slo've:niən]
Montenegro	Montenegro (n)	[mɔnteˈneːgʁo]
Belarus	Weißrussland (n)	['vaɪsˌʁʊslant]
Moldova, Moldavia	Moldawien (n)	[mɔl'daːviən]
Russia	Russland (n)	['ʁʊslant]
Ukraine	Ukraine (f)	[ˌukʁaˈiːnə]

20. Countries of the world. Part 2

Asia	Asien (n)	['aːziən]
Vietnam	Vietnam (n)	[vɪɛt'nam]
India	Indien (n)	['ɪndiən]
Israel	Israel (n)	['ɪsʁaeːl]
China	China (n)	['çiːna]

Lebanon	Libanon (m, n)	['liːbanɔn]
Mongolia	Mongolei (f)	[ˌmɔŋgo'laɪ]
Malaysia	Malaysia (n)	[ma'laɪzɪa]

| Pakistan | **Pakistan** (n) | ['pa:kɪsta:n] |
| Saudi Arabia | **Saudi-Arabien** (n) | [ˌzaʊdiʔaˈʀa:bɪən] |

Thailand	**Thailand** (n)	['taɪlant]
Taiwan	**Taiwan** (n)	[taɪ'va:n]
Turkey	**Türkei** (f)	[tʏʁ'kaɪ]
Japan	**Japan** (n)	['ja:pan]
Afghanistan	**Afghanistan** (n)	[afˈga:nɪsta:n]

Bangladesh	**Bangladesch** (n)	[ˌbaŋglaˈdɛʃ]
Indonesia	**Indonesien** (n)	[ɪndoˈne:zɪən]
Jordan	**Jordanien** (n)	[jɔʁ'da:nɪən]
Iraq	**Irak** (m, n)	[i'ʀa:k]
Iran	**Iran** (m, n)	[i'ʀa:n]

Cambodia	**Kambodscha** (n)	[kam'bɔdʒa]
Kuwait	**Kuwait** (n)	[ku'vaɪt]
Laos	**Laos** (n)	['la:ɔs]
Myanmar	**Myanmar** (n)	['mɪanma:ʁ]
Nepal	**Nepal** (n)	['ne:pal]

United Arab Emirates	**Vereinigten Arabischen Emirate** (pl)	[fɛɛˈʔaɪnɪgən aˈʀa:bɪʃən emiˈʀa:tə]
Syria	**Syrien** (n)	['zy:ʀɪən]
Palestine	**Palästina** (n)	[palɛs'ti:na]
South Korea	**Südkorea** (n)	['zy:tkoˈʀe:a]
North Korea	**Nordkorea** (n)	['nɔʁt·koˈʀe:a]

United States of America	**Die Vereinigten Staaten**	[di fɛɛˈʔaɪnɪçtən 'ʃta:tən]
Canada	**Kanada** (n)	['kanada]
Mexico	**Mexiko** (n)	['mɛksiko:]
Argentina	**Argentinien** (n)	[ˌaʁgɛn'ti:nien]
Brazil	**Brasilien** (n)	[bʀa'zi:lɪən]

Colombia	**Kolumbien** (n)	[ko'lʊmbɪən]
Cuba	**Kuba** (n)	['ku:ba]
Chile	**Chile** (n)	['tʃi:lə]
Venezuela	**Venezuela** (n)	[ˌvene'tsue:la]
Ecuador	**Ecuador** (n)	[ˌekua'do:ʁ]

The Bahamas	**Die Bahamas**	[di ba'ha:ma:s]
Panama	**Panama** (n)	['panama:]
Egypt	**Ägypten** (n)	[ɛ'gʏptən]
Morocco	**Marokko** (n)	[ˌma'ʀɔko]
Tunisia	**Tunesien** (n)	[tu'ne:zɪən]

Kenya	**Kenia** (n)	['ke:nia]
Libya	**Libyen** (n)	['li:byən]
South Africa	**Republik Südafrika** (f)	[ʀepuˈbli:k zy:t̩ʔaːfʀika]
Australia	**Australien** (n)	[aʊsˈtʀa:lɪən]
New Zealand	**Neuseeland** (n)	[nɔɪ'ze:lant]

21. Weather. Natural disasters

weather	Wetter (n)	['vɛtə]
weather forecast	Wetterbericht (m)	['vɛtəbə‚ʀɪçt]
temperature	Temperatur (f)	[tɛmpəʀa'tu:ɐ]
thermometer	Thermometer (n)	[tɛʁmo'me:tɐ]
barometer	Barometer (n)	[baʀo'me:tɐ]

sun	Sonne (f)	['zɔnə]
to shine (vi)	scheinen (vi)	['ʃaɪnən]
sunny (day)	sonnig	['zɔnɪç]
to come up (vi)	aufgehen (vi)	['aʊf‚ge:ən]
to set (vi)	untergehen (vi)	['ʊntɐ‚ge:ən]

rain	Regen (m)	['ʀe:gən]
it's raining	Es regnet	[ɛs 'ʀe:gnət]
pouring rain	strömender Regen (m)	['ʃtʀø:məntdə 'ʀe:gən]
rain cloud	Regenwolke (f)	['ʀe:gən‚vɔlkə]
puddle	Pfütze (f)	['pfʏtsə]
to get wet (in rain)	nass werden (vi)	[nas 've:ɐdən]

thunderstorm	Gewitter (n)	[gə'vɪtɐ]
lightning (~ strike)	Blitz (m)	[blɪts]
to flash (vi)	blitzen (vi)	['blɪtsən]
thunder	Donner (m)	['dɔnɐ]
it's thundering	Es donnert	[ɛs 'dɔnɐt]
hail	Hagel (m)	['ha:gəl]
it's hailing	Es hagelt	[ɛs 'ha:gəlt]

heat (extreme ~)	Hitze (f)	['hɪtsə]
it's hot	ist heiß	[ist haɪs]
it's warm	ist warm	[ist vaʁm]
it's cold	ist kalt	[ist kalt]

fog (mist)	Nebel (m)	['ne:bəl]
foggy	neblig	['ne:blɪç]
cloud	Wolke (f)	['vɔlkə]
cloudy (adj)	bewölkt	[bə'vœlkt]
humidity	Feuchtigkeit (f)	['fɔɪçtɪçkaɪt]

snow	Schnee (m)	[ʃne:]
it's snowing	Es schneit	[ɛs 'ʃnaɪt]
frost (severe ~, freezing cold)	Frost (m)	[fʀɔst]
below zero (adv)	unter Null	['ʊntɐ 'nʊl]
hoarfrost	Reif (m)	[ʀaɪf]

bad weather	Unwetter (n)	['ʊn‚vɛtɐ]
disaster	Katastrophe (f)	[‚katas'tʀo:fə]
flood, inundation	Überschwemmung (f)	[y:bə'ʃvɛmʊŋ]
avalanche	Lawine (f)	[la'vi:nə]

earthquake	Erdbeben (n)	['e:ɛt‚be:bən]
tremor, quake	Erschütterung (f)	[ɛɐ'ʃʏtəʀʊŋ]
epicenter	Epizentrum (n)	[‚epi'tsɛntʀʊm]
eruption	Ausbruch (m)	['aʊs‚bʀʊχ]
lava	Lava (f)	['la:va]

tornado	Tornado (m)	[tɔɐ'na:do]
twister	Wirbelsturm (m)	['vɪʀbəlˌʃtʊʀm]
hurricane	Orkan (m)	[ɔʀ'ka:n]
tsunami	Tsunami (m)	[tsu'na:mi]
cyclone	Zyklon (m)	[tsy'klo:n]

22. Animals. Part 1

| animal | Tier (n) | [ti:ɐ] |
| predator | Raubtier (n) | ['ʀaʊpti:ɐ] |

tiger	Tiger (m)	['ti:gɐ]
lion	Löwe (m)	['lø:və]
wolf	Wolf (m)	[vɔlf]
fox	Fuchs (m)	[fʊks]
jaguar	Jaguar (m)	['ja:gua:ɐ]

lynx	Luchs (m)	[lʊks]
coyote	Kojote (m)	[kɔ'jo:tə]
jackal	Schakal (m)	[ʃa'ka:l]
hyena	Hyäne (f)	['hyɛ:nə]

squirrel	Eichhörnchen (n)	['aɪçˌhœʀnçən]
hedgehog	Igel (m)	['i:gəl]
rabbit	Kaninchen (n)	[ka'ni:nçən]
raccoon	Waschbär (m)	['vaʃˌbɛ:ɐ]

hamster	Hamster (m)	['hamstɐ]
mole	Maulwurf (m)	['maʊlˌvʊʀf]
mouse	Maus (f)	[maʊs]
rat	Ratte (f)	['ʀatə]
bat	Fledermaus (f)	['fle:dɐˌmaʊs]

beaver	Biber (m)	['bi:bɐ]
horse	Pferd (n)	[pfe:ɐt]
deer	Hirsch (m)	[hɪʀʃ]
camel	Kamel (n)	[ka'me:l]
zebra	Zebra (n)	['tse:bʀa]

whale	Wal (m)	[va:l]
seal	Seehund (m)	['ze:ˌhʊnt]
walrus	Walroß (m)	['va:lˌʀɔs]
dolphin	Delfin (m)	[dɛl'fi:n]
bear	Bär (m)	[bɛ:ɐ]

monkey	Affe (m)	['afə]
elephant	Elefant (m)	[ele'fant]
rhinoceros	Nashorn (n)	['naːsˌhɔʁn]
giraffe	Giraffe (f)	[ˌgiˈʁafə]

hippopotamus	Flusspferd (n)	['flʊsˌpfeːɐt]
kangaroo	Känguru (n)	['kɛŋguʁu]
cat	Katze (f)	['katsə]
dog	Hund (m)	[hʊnt]

cow	Kuh (f)	[kuː]
bull	Stier (m)	[ʃtiːɐ]
sheep (ewe)	Schaf (n)	[ʃaːf]
goat	Ziege (f)	['tsiːgə]

donkey	Esel (m)	['eːzəl]
pig, hog	Schwein (n)	[ʃvaɪn]
hen (chicken)	Huhn (n)	[huːn]
rooster	Hahn (m)	[haːn]

duck	Ente (f)	['ɛntə]
goose	Gans (f)	[gans]
turkey (hen)	Pute (f)	['puːtə]
sheepdog	Schäferhund (m)	['ʃɛːfɐˌhʊnt]

23. Animals. Part 2

bird	Vogel (m)	['foːgəl]
pigeon	Taube (f)	['taʊbə]
sparrow	Spatz (m)	[ʃpats]
tit (great tit)	Meise (f)	['maɪzə]
magpie	Elster (f)	['ɛlstɐ]

eagle	Adler (m)	['aːdlɐ]
hawk	Habicht (m)	['haːbɪçt]
falcon	Falke (m)	['falkə]

swan	Schwan (m)	[ʃvaːn]
crane	Kranich (m)	['kʁaːnɪç]
stork	Storch (m)	[ʃtɔʁç]
parrot	Papagei (m)	[papa'gaɪ]
peacock	Pfau (m)	[pfaʊ]
ostrich	Strauß (m)	[ʃtʁaʊs]

heron	Reiher (m)	['ʁaɪɐ]
nightingale	Nachtigall (f)	['naxtɪgal]
swallow	Schwalbe (f)	['ʃvalbə]
woodpecker	Specht (m)	[ʃpɛçt]
cuckoo	Kuckuck (m)	['kʊkʊk]
owl	Eule (f)	['ɔɪlə]

penguin	Pinguin (m)	['pɪŋguiːn]
tuna	Tunfisch (m)	['tuːnfɪʃ]
trout	Forelle (f)	[ˌfoˈʀɛlə]
eel	Aal (m)	[aːl]

shark	Hai (m)	[haɪ]
crab	Krabbe (f)	['kʀabə]
jellyfish	Meduse (f)	[meˈduːzə]
octopus	Krake (m)	['kʀaːkə]

starfish	Seestern (m)	['zeːˌʃtɛʀn]
sea urchin	Seeigel (m)	['zeːˌʔiːgəl]
seahorse	Seepferdchen (n)	['zeːˌpfeːɐtçən]
shrimp	Garnele (f)	[gaʀˈneːlə]

snake	Schlange (f)	['ʃlaŋə]
viper	Viper (f)	['viːpɐ]
lizard	Eidechse (f)	['aɪdɛksə]
iguana	Leguan (m)	['leːguaːn]
chameleon	Chamäleon (n)	[kaˈmɛːleˌɔn]
scorpion	Skorpion (m)	[skɔʀˈpjoːn]

turtle	Schildkröte (f)	['ʃɪltˌkʀøːtə]
frog	Frosch (m)	[fʀɔʃ]
crocodile	Krokodil (n)	[kʀokoˈdiːl]

insect, bug	Insekt (n)	[ɪnˈzɛkt]
butterfly	Schmetterling (m)	['ʃmɛtɐlɪŋ]
ant	Ameise (f)	['aːmaɪzə]
fly	Fliege (f)	['fliːgə]

mosquito	Mücke (f)	['mʏkə]
beetle	Käfer (m)	['kɛːfɐ]
bee	Biene (f)	['biːnə]
spider	Spinne (f)	['ʃpɪnə]

24. Trees. Plants

tree	Baum (m)	[baʊm]
birch	Birke (f)	['bɪʀkə]
oak	Eiche (f)	['aɪçə]
linden tree	Linde (f)	['lɪndə]
aspen	Espe (f)	['ɛspə]

maple	Ahorn (m)	['aːhɔʀn]
spruce	Fichte (f)	['fɪçtə]
pine	Kiefer (f)	['kiːfɐ]
cedar	Zeder (f)	['tseːdɐ]
poplar	Pappel (f)	['papəl]
rowan	Vogelbeerbaum (m)	['foːgəlbeːɐˌbaʊm]

beech	**Buche** (f)	['buːχə]
elm	**Ulme** (f)	['ʊlmə]
ash (tree)	**Esche** (f)	['ɛʃə]
chestnut	**Kastanie** (f)	[kas'taːniə]
palm tree	**Palme** (f)	['palmə]
bush	**Strauch** (m)	[ʃtʀaʊχ]
mushroom	**Pilz** (m)	[pɪlts]
poisonous mushroom	**Giftpilz** (m)	['gɪft͵pɪlts]
cep (Boletus edulis)	**Steinpilz** (m)	['ʃtaɪn͵pɪlts]
russula	**Täubling** (m)	['tɔyplɪŋ]
fly agaric	**Fliegenpilz** (m)	['fliːgən͵pɪlts]
death cap	**Grüner Knollenblätterpilz** (m)	['gʀy:nɐ 'knɔlən·blɛtɐ͵pɪlts]
flower	**Blume** (f)	['bluːmə]
bouquet (of flowers)	**Blumenstrauß** (m)	['bluːmənʃtʀaʊs]
rose (flower)	**Rose** (f)	['ʀoːzə]
tulip	**Tulpe** (f)	['tʊlpə]
carnation	**Nelke** (f)	['nɛlkə]
camomile	**Kamille** (f)	[ka'mɪlə]
cactus	**Kaktus** (m)	['kaktʊs]
lily of the valley	**Maiglöckchen** (n)	['maɪ͵glœkçən]
snowdrop	**Schneeglöckchen** (n)	['ʃneː͵glœkçən]
water lily	**Seerose** (f)	['zeː͵ʀoːzə]
greenhouse (tropical ~)	**Gewächshaus** (n)	[gə'vɛks͵haʊs]
lawn	**Rasen** (m)	['ʀaːzən]
flowerbed	**Beet** (n)	['beːt]
plant	**Pflanze** (f)	['pflantsə]
grass	**Gras** (n)	[gʀaːs]
leaf	**Blatt** (n)	[blat]
petal	**Kelchblatt** (n)	['kɛlç͵blat]
stem	**Stiel** (m)	[ʃtiːl]
young plant (shoot)	**Jungpflanze** (f)	['jʊŋ͵pflantsə]
cereal crops	**Getreidepflanzen** (pl)	[gə'tʀaɪdə͵pflantsən]
wheat	**Weizen** (m)	['vaɪtsən]
rye	**Roggen** (m)	['ʀɔgən]
oats	**Hafer** (m)	['haːfɐ]
millet	**Hirse** (f)	['hɪʀzə]
barley	**Gerste** (f)	['gɛʀstə]
corn	**Mais** (m)	['maɪs]
rice	**Reis** (m)	[ʀaɪs]

25. Various useful words

balance (of situation)	Bilanz (f)	[bi'lants]
base (basis)	Basis (f)	['ba:zɪs]
beginning	Anfang (m)	['anfaŋ]
category	Kategorie (f)	[ˌkatego'ʀi:]
choice	Auswahl (f)	['aʊsva:l]
coincidence	Zufall (m)	['tsu:ˌfal]
comparison	Vergleich (m)	[fɛɐ'glaɪç]
degree (extent, amount)	Grad (m)	[gʀa:t]
development	Entwicklung (f)	[ɛnt'vɪklʊŋ]
difference	Unterschied (m)	['ʊnteʃi:t]
effect (e.g., of drugs)	Effekt (m)	[ɛ'fɛkt]
effort (exertion)	Anstrengung (f)	['anʃtʀɛŋʊŋ]
element	Element (n)	[ele'mɛnt]
example (illustration)	Beispiel (n)	['baɪʃpi:l]
fact	Tatsache (f)	['ta:tˌzaχə]
help	Hilfe (f)	['hɪlfə]
ideal	Ideal (n)	[ide'a:l]
kind (sort, type)	Art (f)	[a:ɐt]
mistake, error	Fehler (m)	['fe:le]
moment	Moment (m)	[mo'mɛnt]
obstacle	Störung (f)	['ʃtø:ʀʊŋ]
part (~ of sth)	Anteil (m)	['anˌtaɪl]
pause (break)	Pause (f)	['paʊzə]
position	Position (f)	[pozi'tsjo:n]
problem	Problem (n)	[pʀo'ble:m]
process	Prozess (m)	[pʀo'tsɛs]
progress	Fortschritt (m)	['foɐtˌʃʀɪt]
property (quality)	Eigenschaft (f)	['aɪgənʃaft]
reaction	Reaktion (f)	[ˌʀeak'tsjo:n]
risk	Risiko (n)	['ʀi:ziko]
secret	Geheimnis (n)	[gə'haɪmnɪs]
series	Serie (f)	['ze:ʀiə]
shape (outer form)	Form (f)	[foɐm]
situation	Situation (f)	[zitua'tsjo:n]
solution	Lösung (f)	['lø:zʊŋ]
standard (adj)	Standard-	['standaɐt]
stop (pause)	Halt (m)	[halt]
style	Stil (m)	[ʃti:l]
system	System (n)	[zʏs'te:m]

table (chart)	**Tabelle** (f)	[ta'bɛlə]
tempo, rate	**Tempo** (n)	['tɛmpo]
term (word, expression)	**Fachwort** (n)	['faχˌvɔʁt]
truth (e.g., moment of ~)	**Wahrheit** (f)	['va:ɐhaɪt]
turn (please wait your ~)	**Reihe** (f)	['ʀaɪə]
urgent (adj)	**dringend**	['dʀɪŋənt]
utility (usefulness)	**Nutzen** (m)	['nʊtsən]
variant (alternative)	**Variante** (f)	[va'ʀɪantə]
way (means, method)	**Weise** (f)	['vaɪzə]
zone	**Zone** (f)	['tso:nə]

26. Modifiers. Adjectives. Part 1

additional (adj)	**ergänzend**	[ɛɐ'gɛntsənt]
ancient (~ civilization)	**alt**	[alt]
artificial (adj)	**künstlich**	['kʏnstlɪç]
bad (adj)	**schlecht**	[ʃlɛçt]
beautiful (person)	**schön**	[ʃø:n]
big (in size)	**groß**	[gʀo:s]
bitter (taste)	**bitter**	['bɪtə]
blind (sightless)	**blind**	[blɪnt]
central (adj)	**zentral**	[tsɛn'tʀa:l]
children's (adj)	**Kinder-**	['kɪndɐ]
clandestine (secret)	**Untergrund-**	['ʊntəˌgʀʊnt]
clean (free from dirt)	**sauber**	['zaʊbɐ]
clever (smart)	**klug**	[klu:k]
compatible (adj)	**kompatibel**	[kɔmpa'ti:bəl]
contented (satisfied)	**zufrieden**	[tsu'fʀi:dən]
dangerous (adj)	**gefährlich**	[gə'fɛ:ɐlɪç]
dead (not alive)	**tot**	[to:t]
dense (fog, smoke)	**dicht**	[dɪçt]
difficult (decision)	**schwierig**	['ʃvi:ʀɪç]
dirty (not clean)	**schmutzig**	['ʃmʊtsɪç]
easy (not difficult)	**einfach**	['aɪnfaχ]
empty (glass, room)	**leer**	[le:ɐ]
exact (amount)	**genau**	[gə'naʊ]
excellent (adj)	**ausgezeichnet**	['aʊsgəˌtsaɪçnət]
excessive (adj)	**übermäßig**	['y:bɐˌmɛ:sɪç]
exterior (adj)	**Außen-, äußer**	['aʊsən], ['ɔɪsɐ]
fast (quick)	**schnell**	[ʃnɛl]
fertile (land, soil)	**fruchtbar**	['fʀʊχtba:ɐ]
fragile (china, glass)	**zerbrechlich**	[tsɛɐ'bʀɛçlɪç]
free (at no cost)	**kostenlos, gratis**	['kɔstənlo:s], ['gʀa:tɪs]

fresh (~ water)	Süß-	[zy:s]
frozen (food)	tiefgekühlt	['ti:fgə͜ky:lt]
full (completely filled)	voll	[fɔl]
happy (adj)	glücklich	['glʏklɪç]

hard (not soft)	hart	[haʁt]
huge (adj)	riesig	['ʀi:zɪç]
ill (sick, unwell)	krank	[kʀaŋk]
immobile (adj)	unbeweglich	['ʊnbə͜ve:klɪç]
important (adj)	wichtig	['vɪçtɪç]

interior (adj)	innen-	['ɪnən]
last (e.g., ~ week)	vorig	['fo:ʀɪç]
last (final)	der letzte	[de:ɐ 'lɛtstə]
left (e.g., ~ side)	link	[lɪŋk]
legal (legitimate)	gesetzlich	[gə'zɛtslɪç]

light (in weight)	leicht	[laɪçt]
liquid (fluid)	flüssig	['flʏsɪç]
long (e.g., ~ hair)	lang	[laŋ]
loud (voice, etc.)	laut	[laʊt]
low (voice)	leise	['laɪzə]

27. Modifiers. Adjectives. Part 2

main (principal)	Haupt-	[haʊpt]
matt, matte	matt	[mat]
mysterious (adj)	rätselhaft	['ʀɛ:tsəl͜haft]
narrow (street, etc.)	eng, schmal	[ɛŋ], [ʃma:l]
native (~ country)	Heimat-	['haɪma:t]

negative (~ response)	negativ	['ne:gati:f]
new (adj)	neu	[nɔɪ]
next (e.g., ~ week)	nächst	[nɛ:çst]
normal (adj)	normal	[nɔʁ'ma:l]
not difficult (adj)	nicht schwierig	[nɪçt 'ʃvi:ʀɪç]

obligatory (adj)	obligatorisch, Pflicht-	[ɔbliga'to:ʀɪʃ], [pflɪçt]
old (house)	alt	[alt]
open (adj)	offen	['ɔfən]
opposite (adj)	gegensätzlich	['ge:gən͜zɛtslɪç]
ordinary (usual)	gewöhnlich	[gə'vø:nlɪç]

original (unusual)	original	[oʀigi'na:l]
personal (adj)	persönlich	[pɛʁ'zø:nlɪç]
polite (adj)	höflich	['hø:flɪç]
poor (not rich)	arm	[aʁm]

| possible (adj) | möglich | ['mø:klɪç] |
| principal (main) | hauptsächlich | ['haʊpt͜zɛçlɪç] |

probable (adj)	wahrscheinlich	[vaːɐ̯ˈʃaɪnlɪç]
prolonged (e.g., ~ applause)	andauernd	[ˈanˌdaʊɐnt]
public (open to all)	öffentlich	[ˈœfəntlɪç]

rare (adj)	selten	[ˈzɛltən]
raw (uncooked)	roh	[ROː]
right (not left)	recht	[RƐçt]
ripe (fruit)	reif	[Raɪf]

risky (adj)	riskant	[Rɪsˈkant]
sad (~ look)	traurig, unglücklich	[ˈtRaʊRɪç], [ˈʊnˌɡlʏklɪç]
second hand (adj)	gebraucht	[ɡəˈbRaʊχt]
shallow (water)	seicht	[zaɪçt]
sharp (blade, etc.)	scharf	[ʃaʁf]

short (in length)	kurz	[kʊʁts]
similar (adj)	ähnlich	[ˈɛːnlɪç]
small (in size)	klein	[klaɪn]
smooth (surface)	glatt	[ɡlat]
soft (~ toys)	weich	[vaɪç]

solid (~ wall)	fest, stark	[fɛst], [ʃtaʁk]
sour (flavor, taste)	sauer	[ˈzaʊɐ]
spacious (house, etc.)	geräumig	[ɡəˈRɔɪmɪç]
special (adj)	speziell, Spezial-	[ʃpeˈtsiɛl], [ʃpeˈtsiaːl]

straight (line, road)	gerade	[ɡəˈRaːdə]
strong (person)	stark	[ʃtaʁk]
stupid (foolish)	dumm	[dʊm]
superb, perfect (adj)	ausgezeichnet	[ˈaʊsɡəˌtsaɪçnət]

sweet (sugary)	süß	[zyːs]
tan (adj)	gebräunt	[ɡəˈbRɔɪnt]
tasty (delicious)	lecker	[ˈlɛkɐ]
unclear (adj)	undeutlich	[ˈʊnˌdɔɪtlɪç]

28. Verbs. Part 1

to accuse (vt)	anklagen (vt)	[ˈanˌklaːɡən]
to agree (say yes)	zustimmen (vi)	[ˈtsuːˌʃtɪmən]
to announce (vt)	anzeigen (vt)	[ˈanˌtsaɪɡən]
to answer (vi, vt)	antworten (vi)	[ˈantˌvɔʁtən]
to apologize (vi)	sich entschuldigen	[zɪç ɛntˈʃʊldɪɡən]

to arrive (vi)	ankommen (vi)	[ˈanˌkɔmən]
to ask (~ oneself)	fragen (vt)	[ˈfRaːɡən]
to be absent	fehlen (vi)	[ˈfeːlən]
to be afraid	Angst haben	[ˈaŋst ˈhaːbən]
to be born	geboren sein	[ɡəˈboːRən zaɪn]

to be in a hurry	sich beeilen	[zɪç bə'ʔaɪlən]
to beat (to hit)	schlagen (vt)	['ʃla:gən]
to begin (vt)	beginnen (vt)	[bə'gɪnən]
to believe (in God)	glauben (vt)	['glaʊbən]
to belong to ...	gehören (vi)	[gə'hø:ʁən]
to break (split into pieces)	brechen (vt)	['bʁɛçən]

to build (vt)	bauen (vt)	['baʊən]
to buy (purchase)	kaufen (vt)	['kaufən]
can (v aux)	können (v mod)	['kœnən]
can (v aux)	können (v mod)	['kœnən]
to cancel (call off)	abschaffen (vt)	['apˌʃafən]

to catch (vt)	fangen (vt)	['faŋən]
to change (vt)	ändern (vt)	['ɛndən]
to check (to examine)	prüfen (vt)	['pʀy:fən]
to choose (select)	wählen (vt)	['vɛ:lən]
to clean up (tidy)	aufräumen (vt)	['aʊfˌʁɔɪmən]

to close (vt)	schließen (vt)	['ʃli:sən]
to compare (vt)	vergleichen (vt)	[fɛɐ'glaɪçən]
to complain (vi, vt)	klagen (vi)	['kla:gən]

| to confirm (vt) | bestätigen (vt) | [bə'ʃtɛ:tɪgən] |
| to congratulate (vt) | gratulieren (vi) | [gʁatu'li:ʁən] |

to cook (dinner)	zubereiten (vt)	['tsu:bəˌʁaɪtən]
to copy (vt)	kopieren (vt)	[ko'pi:ʁən]
to cost (vt)	kosten (vt)	['kɔstən]

| to count (add up) | rechnen (vt) | ['ʁɛçnən] |
| to count on ... | auf ... zählen | [aʊf ... 'tsɛ:lən] |

to create (vt)	schaffen (vt)	['ʃafən]
to cry (weep)	weinen (vi)	['vaɪnən]
to dance (vi, vt)	tanzen (vi, vt)	['tantsən]

| to deceive (vi, vt) | täuschen (vt) | ['tɔɪʃən] |
| to decide (~ to do sth) | entscheiden (vt) | [ɛnt'ʃaɪdən] |

to delete (vt)	löschen (vt)	['lœʃən]
to demand (request firmly)	verlangen (vt)	[fɛɐ'laŋən]
to deny (vt)	verneinen (vt)	[fɛɐ'naɪnən]

| to depend on ... | abhängen von ... | ['apˌhɛŋən fɔn] |
| to despise (vt) | verachten (vt) | [fɛɐ'ʔaxtən] |

to die (vi)	sterben (vi)	['ʃtɛʁbən]
to dig (vt)	graben (vt)	['gʁa:bən]
to disappear (vi)	verschwinden (vi)	[fɛɐ'ʃvɪndən]
to discuss (vt)	besprechen (vt)	[bə'ʃpʁɛçən]
to disturb (vt)	stören (vt)	['ʃtø:ʁən]

29. Verbs. Part 2

to dive (vi)	**tauchen** (vi)	['tauxən]
to divorce (vi)	**sich scheiden lassen**	[zɪç 'ʃaɪdən 'lasən]
to do (vt)	**machen** (vt)	['maxən]
to doubt (have doubts)	**zweifeln** (vi)	['tsvaɪfəln]
to drink (vi, vt)	**trinken** (vt)	['tʀɪŋkən]
to drop (let fall)	**fallen lassen**	['falən 'lasən]
to dry (clothes, hair)	**trocknen** (vt)	['tʀɔknən]
to eat (vi, vt)	**essen** (vi, vt)	['ɛsən]
to end (~ a relationship)	**abbrechen** (vi)	['apˌbʀɛçən]
to excuse (forgive)	**entschuldigen** (vt)	[ɛnt'ʃʊldɪgən]
to exist (vi)	**existieren** (vi)	[ˌɛksɪs'tiːʀən]
to expect (foresee)	**voraussehen** (vt)	[fo'ʀaʊsˌzeːən]
to explain (vt)	**erklären** (vt)	[ɛɐ'klɛːʀən]
to fall (vi)	**fallen** (vi)	['falən]
to fight (street fight, etc.)	**sich prügeln**	[zɪç 'pʀyːgəln]
to find (vt)	**finden** (vt)	['fɪndən]
to finish (vt)	**beenden** (vt)	[bə'ʔɛndən]
to fly (vi)	**fliegen** (vi)	['fliːgən]
to forbid (vt)	**verbieten** (vt)	[fɛɐ'biːtən]
to forget (vi, vt)	**vergessen** (vt)	[fɛɐ'gɛsən]
to forgive (vt)	**verzeihen** (vt)	[fɛɐ'tsaɪən]
to get tired	**müde werden**	['myːdə 'veːɐdən]
to give (vt)	**geben** (vt)	['geːbən]
to go (on foot)	**gehen** (vi)	['geːən]
to hate (vt)	**hassen** (vt)	['hasən]
to have (vt)	**haben** (vt)	[haːbən]
to have breakfast	**frühstücken** (vi)	['fʀyːˌʃtʏkən]
to have dinner	**zu Abend essen**	[tsu 'aːbənt 'ɛsən]
to have lunch	**zu Mittag essen**	[tsu 'mɪtaːk 'ɛsən]
to hear (vt)	**hören** (vt)	['høːʀən]
to help (vt)	**helfen** (vi)	['hɛlfən]
to hide (vt)	**verstecken** (vt)	[fɛɐ'ʃtɛkən]
to hope (vi, vt)	**hoffen** (vi)	['hɔfən]
to hunt (vi, vt)	**jagen** (vi)	['jagən]
to hurry (vi)	**sich beeilen**	[zɪç bə'ʔaɪlən]
to insist (vi, vt)	**bestehen** (vi)	[bə'ʃteːən]
to insult (vt)	**kränken** (vt)	['kʀɛŋkən]
to invite (vt)	**einladen** (vt)	['aɪnˌlaːdən]
to joke (vi)	**Witz machen**	[vɪts 'maxən]
to keep (vt)	**aufbewahren** (vt)	['aʊfbəˌvaːʀən]
to kill (vt)	**ermorden** (vt)	[ɛɐ'mɔʀdən]
to know (sb)	**kennen** (vt)	['kɛnən]

to know (sth)	**wissen** (vt)	['vɪsən]
to like (I like …)	**gefallen** (vi)	[ɡə'falən]
to look at …	**ansehen** (vt)	['anze:ən]
to lose (umbrella, etc.)	**verlieren** (vt)	[fɛɐ'li:ʀən]
to love (sb)	**lieben** (vt)	['li:bən]
to make a mistake	**sich irren**	[zɪç 'ɪʀən]
to meet (vi, vt)	**sich treffen**	[zɪç 'tʀɛfən]
to miss (school, etc.)	**versäumen** (vt)	[fɛɐ'zɔɪmən]

30. Verbs. Part 3

to obey (vi, vt)	**gehorchen** (vi)	[ɡə'hɔʀçən]
to open (vt)	**öffnen** (vt)	['œfnən]
to participate (vi)	**teilnehmen** (vi)	['taɪl‚ne:mən]
to pay (vi, vt)	**zahlen** (vt)	['tsa:lən]
to permit (vt)	**erlauben** (vt)	[ɛɐ'laʊbən]
to play (children)	**spielen** (vi, vt)	['ʃpi:lən]
to pray (vi, vt)	**beten** (vi)	['be:tən]
to promise (vt)	**versprechen** (vt)	[fɛɐ'ʃpʀɛçən]
to propose (vt)	**vorschlagen** (vt)	['fo:ɐ‚ʃla:ɡən]
to prove (vt)	**beweisen** (vt)	[bə'vaɪzən]
to read (vi, vt)	**lesen** (vi, vt)	['le:zən]
to receive (vt)	**bekommen** (vt)	[bə'kɔmən]
to rent (sth from sb)	**mieten** (vt)	['mi:tən]
to repeat (say again)	**noch einmal sagen**	[nɔx 'aɪnma:l 'za:ɡən]
to reserve, to book	**reservieren** (vt)	[ʀezɛɐ'vi:ʀən]
to run (vi)	**laufen** (vi)	['laʊfən]
to save (rescue)	**retten** (vt)	['ʀɛtən]
to say (~ thank you)	**sagen** (vt)	['za:ɡən]
to see (vt)	**sehen** (vi, vt)	['ze:ən]
to sell (vt)	**verkaufen** (vt)	[fɛɐ'kaʊfən]
to send (vt)	**abschicken** (vt)	['ap‚ʃɪkən]
to shoot (vi)	**schießen** (vi)	['ʃi:sən]
to shout (vi)	**schreien** (vi)	['ʃʀaɪən]
to show (vt)	**zeigen** (vt)	['tsaɪɡən]
to sign (document)	**unterschreiben** (vt)	[‚ʊntɐ'ʃʀaɪbən]
to sing (vi)	**singen** (vt)	['zɪŋən]
to sit down (vi)	**sich setzen**	[zɪç 'zɛtsən]
to smile (vi)	**lächeln** (vi)	['lɛçəln]
to speak (vi, vt)	**sprechen** (vi)	['ʃpʀɛçən]
to steal (money, etc.)	**stehlen** (vt)	['ʃte:lən]
to stop (please ~ calling me)	**einstellen** (vt)	['aɪn‚ʃtɛlən]
to study (vt)	**lernen** (vt)	['lɛʀnən]

to swim (vi)	schwimmen (vi)	['ʃvɪmən]
to take (vt)	nehmen (vt)	['neːmən]
to talk to ...	sprechen mit ...	['ʃpʀɛçən mɪt]
to tell (story, joke)	erzählen (vt)	[ɛɐ̯'tsɛːlən]
to thank (vt)	danken (vi)	['daŋkən]
to think (vi, vt)	denken (vi, vt)	['dɛŋkən]

to translate (vt)	übersetzen (vt)	[ˌyːbɐ'zɛtsən]
to trust (vt)	vertrauen (vi)	[fɛɐ̯'tʀaʊən]
to try (attempt)	versuchen (vt)	[fɛɐ̯'zuːxən]
to turn (e.g., ~ left)	abbiegen (vi)	['apˌbiːgən]
to turn off	ausschalten (vt)	['aʊsˌʃaltən]

to turn on	einschalten (vt)	['aɪnˌʃaltən]
to understand (vt)	verstehen (vt)	[fɛɐ̯'ʃteːən]
to wait (vt)	warten (vi)	['vaʁtən]
to want (wish, desire)	wollen (vt)	['vɔlən]
to work (vi)	arbeiten (vi)	['aʁbaɪtən]
to write (vt)	schreiben (vi, vt)	['ʃʀaɪbən]

www.ingramcontent.com/pod-product-compliance
Lightning Source LLC
Chambersburg PA
CBHW060023050426

42448CB00012B/2855